Synagogue and Church in the Middle Ages:
Two Symbols in Art and Literature

Synagogue and Church in the Middle Ages:

Two Symbols in Art and Literature

WOLFGANG S. SEIFERTH

Translated by Lee Chadeayne and Paul Gottwald

Frederick Ungar Publishing Co.
New York

Translated from the German *Synagoge und Kirche im Mittelalter*
by arrangement with Kösel-Verlag KG., Munich

Printed in the United States of America
Library of Congress Catalog Card Number: 75-107031
ISBN 0-8044-5870-7

Contents

Preface

The destinies of the synagogue and church can be traced through about fifteen centuries of Christian history. If, in addition, we investigate the origins of their respective symbolic representations in the Old Testament, this period is enlarged to far more than two millennia. Like an often invisible yet unbroken thread, the history of the relationship between Judaism and Christianity runs down through the Christian era and into the present.

Almost as vast as the period of time involved is the diversity of meanings embodied in the two figures of Synagoga and Ecclesia—especially the former. This multiplicity reaches all the way from the authority of the Bible and the church fathers to ordinary prejudice, contempt, and hatred; often the assertion remains fragmentary or ambiguous. The figures representing church and synagogue appear at the portals of medieval cathedrals in the company of kings, patriarchs, apostles, and saints; but whereas the latter figures are clearly articulated by name, biblical quotation, and legend, the dialogue between Ecclesia and Synagoga remains inaudible and can only be inferred from long-forgotten sources of quite another sort—literature, sermons and tracts, and social history. The study of the complex and often contradictory iconography of the two figures must therefore be broadened into a thoroughgoing examination of the culture, which will nevertheless still leave a number of unanswered questions.

The Jesuit fathers Cahier and Martin were the first to investigate systematically the allegories of Ecclesia and Synagoga. In their monumental work concerning the stained-glass windows of the Bourges Cathedral, which appeared between 1841 and 1844, they assembled pertinent passages from the Bible, patristic writings, and church doctrine, thereby establishing the basis for further research. Fifty years later, Paul Weber, with his knowledge of the medieval drama, was able to add to this material in his study that sought to determine more precisely the relationship between clerical drama and church art. He saw in the two female figures the principal theme of Christian religion and art; he was also the first to depict this theme against the somber background of medieval Jewish history. The religious communality of the two figures, their service to a higher ideal, was emphasized especially by Franz Xaver Kraus and later by Joseph Sauer. The most important source for the art historian is found in A. Goldschmidt's magnificent collection of plates, where the first artistic flowering of the theme in ivory carvings is depicted as completely as possible in numerous illustrations.

The formal aesthetics that predominated in the art history of the 1920s was not interested in the revelation of symbols and logical relationships, and narrow specialization rendered a comprehensive view more difficult. Only the last forty years of German history have clearly revealed to us the central significance of church and synagogue in the totality of the historical world. In each chapter of this book the reader will rediscover the thematic connection between our age and these medieval allegories. For the author, this discovery carried with it the challenge to reexamine the existing material, supplement it with personal investigation, and place it before the contemporary public.

This work could not have been completed without the generous assistance of Howard University, where I have been a member of the faculty since 1937. I wish to express my gratitude to the University for the grants that helped me to pursue my research abroad and for its contribution toward the production of the photographic plates in 1964. In addition, special thanks are extended to the various museums, libraries, and institutions that have granted reproduction rights for the illustrations.

The American edition is a faithful rendering of the German original except that Chapters 9 and 10 contain some additional material. For the English text of quotations from the Bible, the translators have used the equivalents from the Revised Standard Version.

This American edition became possible primarily through the initiative of the publisher Frederick Ungar, New York, and through the assistance rendered by Howard University in sharing the translation expenses.

—Wolfgang S. Seiferth

Washington, D.C.
Summer 1969

Chapter 1

The Women at the Foot of the Cross

Were you there when they crucified my Lord?
Were you there when the sun refused to shine?
—NEGRO SPIRITUAL

I

The National Library in Paris preserves a prayer book dating from the ninth century, the Sacramentary of Drogo. Drogo was the name of its owner, a son of Charlemagne, who was Bishop of Metz about the middle of the century. Among the prayers for Holy Week there is an illustration of Christ's crucifixion inserted within the circle of the letter *O* (Fig. 1). At the foot of the cross stands the figure of a woman with a banner, holding aloft a chalice in her right hand to receive the blood of Christ. Ecclesia, the Christian church, receives her mission and authority from Christ in the hour of his death.

This letter *O* contains the first ascertainable portrayal of Ecclesia at the foot of the cross. In the golden splendor of the halo, the banner, and the chalice, she renders her symbolic service to the Savior.

The crucifixion was a relatively late pictorial theme. Early examples are isolated (the door of Santa Sabina in Rome, about 430; a mural in Santa Maria Antica in Rome, sixth century). Since Carolingian times, however, the crucifixion has become well established in Christian art. Later, the portrayal of the crucifixion combined with other biblical themes, such as the creation, the fall of man, and the last judgment. Since the time of Drogo's Sacramentary, the allegorical female figures Ecclesia and Synagoga are also a part of the crucifixion scene. They have the possibility of making theological statements that broaden in medieval art to a major artistic theme.

Such a representation is by no means self-evident. An image derived from a historical event–the crucifixion of Christ–combined with figures that stand not for themselves but for a reality that can be only intellectually comprehended and that is personified in them, thus becoming visible and active. The "allegory," with its relationship to a historical moment, was an essential means of expression in the art of the Roman Empire and contributed to its speculative character. Thus we find, for example, two female figures on the relief armor of the famous statue of Augustus at Primaporta as symbols for two conquered provinces.

This allegorical manner of expression was taken over into early Christian art along with the pictorial style of the late period of the empire. As the "orant," the female figure became a principal motif in the catacomb paintings. Originally, she probably stood for the deceased as intercessor for the living, but this significance as intercessor was soon broadened and she became the Mother of God or the incarnation of the church. As early as the first half of the fifth century she appeared as Ecclesia on the wooden door of Santa Sabina. There she is placed between Peter and Paul, who crown her with the sign of Christ.

This combination of allegory and history requires a pictorial style that removes the event portrayed from its realistic and historical context. Through the use of symbolic devices as applied to space, color references, arrangement of figures according to rank, and gestures, the event was incorporated into a reality not bounded by time in which it merged with the allegorical elements. This pictorial style also developed in the late Roman period and became a significant basis for the art of the Middle Ages.

The crucifixion scene in the initial *O* of Drogo's Sacramentary also appears in this symbolic dimension. Sitting opposite Ecclesia is an old man with white hair. Somewhat removed from the cross, he is raising his right hand and holding a symbol of authority in his left. In contrast with the decisive way in which Ecclesia faces the cross, his attitude seems passive and listless. He probably was intended to represent Judaism, which Christ turned away from in conferring succession upon Ecclesia with his blood. But the three figures belong inseparably together, forming a symmetrical composition: the rust-red in Christ's loincloth reappears in Ecclesia's mantle and in the lower garment of the old man. For the first time the religious conflict between Judaism and Christianity was formulated in a manner that set the style for centuries; but we also find an intimate connection between the Old and the New Covenant. Its representatives are brought together at the foot of the cross and are separated from one another by it.

In the Nikasius diptych in Tournai (ca. 900) the theme was pursued further (Fig. 2). The place of the old man is taken by a second female figure, and both women are mentioned by name for the first time: Santa Ecclesia and Hierusalem. Outwardly they are scarcely differentiated: the garments allow only the face and hands to be revealed; the border of the mantle is drawn over the head in the classical manner. But the second figure expresses helplessness and consternation as she looks up at Christ—*Hic est Jesus Nazarenus Rex Judaeorum*—at the chalice, and at the darkening sun and moon. Behind her, at the edge, there are walls with spires—probably an abbreviation for the city of Jerusalem—while behind Ecclesia stands the symbol of a romanesque church.

On several ivory book covers (dating from the ninth and tenth centuries), which, like Drogo's Sacramentary, originated in a workshop in Metz, the theme of Ecclesia and Synagoga for the first time acquired a clear form and, evidently, wider distribution than we are able to prove today. Ancient Lotharingia, the capital of which was Metz, was in the heart of the Carolingian Empire. Remains of Roman city culture had survived the Great Migration, and the episcopal churches in this region were conscious of their origin in the early Christian era. Creative forces from the East and West came together here in a new union before the destinies of the German and French nations went their separate ways. Ecclesia and Synagoga were part of the intellectual and formal treasury of this early, pre-national epoch in Europe and appear in the forms and framework of the late Roman pictorial tradition.

Among the creations of this workshop in Metz, four ivory tablets (now in Paris, Gannat, London, and Metz) are especially closely related in idea, arrangement, and technique, and can be considered as one group.[1] In each case a large cross stands in the middle of the composition with the two female figures below it. Other events in the passion of Christ are depicted with additional allegorical figures on several tiers (Figs. 3 and 4).

While Ecclesia performs her sacred duty, Synagoga, leaning on her banner, turns away and prepares to leave—yet her gaze remains fixed on the crucified Christ. Mary and John are larger than the two women and flank the central group. On the tier below stands the captain Longinus with lance raised; opposite him is the soldier Stephaton with his reed and sponge soaked in vinegar. Tombs open and discharge their dead. Sun and moon, angels and men, the dead and the living, and Oceanus and Gaea assemble as witnesses in the hour of Christ's death. Synagoga alone seems to be unwilling to recognize the man on the cross as the Savior. She stands apart: in the presence of all of creation she is dispossessed of her venerable and historic mission as bearer of God's word. Her authority devolves on Ecclesia, who is collecting the precious blood of the Savior in a jug. This jug, which later becomes a chalice, is one of Ecclesia's symbols.

The tablets in Paris and in Gannat show, in addition, the appearance of the women at the tomb on Easter morning.

All the tablets in this group contain a wealth of formal elements derived from antiquity. The field is enclosed in an acanthus frame. On Adalbero's tablet (Fig. 4) the cross rises above a magnificent column whose capital portrays the fall of man: the cross, the new tree of life, grows out of the tree of knowledge between Adam and Eve. The lower tiers contain figures representing the four Evangelists as well as Oceanus and Gaea. Engraved in the base of the column is a picture of the patron and owner, Adalbero II, Bishop of Metz—a biographical document unusual in that time.

On all the tablets in this group Ecclesia and Synagoga

differ outwardly only in their movements and in the different symbols of their office–not in their position, form, or dress. Only on the London tablet does Ecclesia have a halo as in Drogo's Sacramentary. Synagoga appears undaunted and with banner fluttering. The portrayal can be read like a text; Synagoga is the forerunner, Ecclesia the fulfillment. Each of the two women stands at her own particular stage of revelation; the first must go when the time is fulfilled, and the second comes. "But now that faith has come, we are no longer under a custodian" of the law, as Paul writes to the Galatians (3:25). The law of the Old Covenant is surmounted and superseded at the cross by God's love. The two figures appear symbolically as members of a higher unity, the concept of God, which grows in the course of history and is revealed in stages.

II

The inner unity of the women at the foot of the cross did not remain undisturbed. On other ivory tablets from the same period,[2] which did not come from Metz but nevertheless are within the same sphere of ideas, the beginnings of an estrangement between the two figures can be seen. The composition in the tablets became more elaborate and less static, and the scene at the foot of the cross was dramatically intensified. The imagination overstepped the bounds of the old symbol and formulated, along with the gradually unfolding religious idea, other experiences of a quite different sort.

The ivory tablet from the treasury of the Bamberg Cathedral (Fig. 5) was carved about the year 870, and about 140 years later Heinrich II chose it as a book cover for the precious evangelistary that he donated to the Bamberg Cathedral, his favorite foundation. The rigid order is relaxed by a flowing composition with considerable depth effect; the wooden arrangement of the figures gives way to dramatic scenes. The great skill of the carver revealed rich details in every figure without losing sight of the context. Ecclesia appears twice: first with the chalice in the *unio mystica* at the foot of the cross, then in the disputation with Synagoga that is common to the three tablets in this group. Below, between Oceanus and Gaea, the figure of Roma is enthroned: the ruler of the ancient world is thus also a witness of Christ's death on the cross. The dead emerge from their tombs. The Easter cycle is enlarged showing the three women, the angel seated before the enormous tomb, and behind it, small and crowded against the edge, the sleeping watchmen. "Freedom of mobility prevails in the figures . . . , the three angels above the cross are very skillfully grouped; in the case of the figures rising from the dead both the anatomy of the naked body and the covering of the shroud are exceptionally well executed" (Goldschmidt).

Several scenes take place around the cross. Ecclesia receives the blood of the Savior, the chalice replacing the jug of older ivory tablets. Christ turns his head toward her. The soldier pierces His side with a spear while five grieving women stand at one side. On the other side of the cross John and Stephaton balance the figures of Ecclesia and the soldier. At the top of the tablet the hand of God shows the angels the way to the cross, and sun and moon ride across the sky in their classical vehicles.

On the right side a scene takes place that is slightly modified in the other two tablets. Synagoga sits in front of her temple with a crown on her head and a globe of the earth in her hand. Ecclesia, her banner fluttering, steps up to her and lays hands on the globe. Just as in the transmittal of a fief in medieval law, Ecclesia, the assignee, takes possession of the house, office, and rank of her predecessor. However, this takes place without triumph or humiliation: Synagoga is a queen and one of the tablets (London) even has a soldier standing guard at her side. Just as on Hadrian's coins the earth, Gaea, is portrayed as an illustrious woman by means of a crown resembling a city wall on her head, here too Jerusalem the Queen appears with the symbols of her authority. The scene is symbolic, but the symbol was no longer exclusively religious. Along with the original idea, secular thoughts had entered. Claims to authority are adjudicated, legal and ritual symbols appear. The estrangement produces a distinct contrast: the beginnings of the disputation between Ecclesia and Synagoga, which continued in the centuries to follow.

The book cover of the Codex Latinus 9383 in Paris (Fig. 6) likewise reveals the great skill of its creator. He, too, used the traditional grouping for his own ideas. Ecclesia appears only in the disputation on the right side. As legal successor she seizes property and office from Jerusalem the Queen, whose head is enclosed, as if by a halo, in a wreath resembling the city wall of Jerusalem.

Ecclesia is smaller than her mighty predecessor. With one hand she points to Synagoga's forehead, indicating that the source of salvation will be there in the future and not in the knife of circumcision, which Synagoga holds in her left hand. The gods of antiquity at the bottom of the tablet are drawn to the crucifixion with great expressiveness. Roma is enthroned at the foot of the cross, the banner and globe of the earth in her hands; she had become equal in significance to Synagoga. Mary stands at the foot of the cross in Ecclesia's usual place. With open eyes Christ says, "Mother, this is thy son." John is ready to take the Lord's mother into his care. In the faces of the four evangelists is earnest certainty; visions guide their hands as they write. The three winged beasts of the Gospels and the angel of John rush down from above like a divine revelation.

The third tablet in this group (London) portrays a disputation in the right half of the picture as do the two other tablets. Beside Synagoga stands an armed soldier, stressing her regal position. In idea and execution this tablet is of lesser quality. Also—as can often be shown in second-rate works—it appears to contain an error: Ecclesia holds a trident in her hands instead of her banner.

III

Finally, the theme underwent further, fundamental modifications. The estrangement grew, the symmetry of the two figures was disturbed, and their higher unity jeopardized. The composition of the tablet in the Bargello in Florence, dating from the tenth century (Fig. 7; Goldschmidt I, No. 114), has little in common with the older ivory tablets of the Metz school. Ecclesia, standing between Mary and Longinus, wears a crown over her loosely falling hair. Synagoga has already given up her important place at the foot of the Cross, is crowded against the edge of the picture on the right and is leaving the crucifixion scene. Bareheaded and without her banner she turns away from the dominant crucifix. Sun and moon have exchanged their traditional places.

The equally unusual composition of a tablet (London)[3] made in the eleventh century in Cologne documents the further changes that occurred in the concept of Ecclesia and Synagoga. Here the role of Ecclesia had devolved on a man, and Synagoga as well is represented by a man who shrinks back in astonishment, thus preserving her gesture. Synagoga is completely displaced from the middle of the picture, appearing as a half-figure in the lower right-hand corner. She covers one eye plaintively with her left hand, and in her right hand holds a lance with a bent point, the earliest example of this significant symbol. In the left-hand corner of the picture appears her counterpart, a man raising his hands in prayer.

No new, general pattern was visible yet in the broken symmetry and in the sharp conflict between belief and disbelief, between communion with God and repudiation. The last two examples are in pronounced contrast with the ivory tablets in the first group. The original symbols of divine revelation in the Old and the New Covenants—seen in the equal rank of the women at the cross—had been joined by symbols of dominion and power, which finally seemed to suggest the rejection of the Old Covenant. The new symbols ushered in changes. Synagoga had lost her position by the cross. A new clarification of the content was under way and was formulated in the romanesque miniatures.

Typical of these didactic efforts is the crucifixion scene in the evangelistary of the abbess Uta of Niedermünster (Fig. 10).[4] The work was written and illustrated in the early eleventh century in Regensburg. The crucifixion scene is composed of allegorical figures, quotations, and even musical symbols in a framework of lines and planes; its historical significance was interpreted in a graphic system.

The cross divides the composition into two equal halves. On Jesus's right, in the picture border, we find the symbols of grace and salvation: the sun, Ecclesia, and a resurrection scene. At the foot of the cross, again to Jesus's right, stands the carefully drawn figure of a woman with a crown: the personification of Life. Her bright garment makes her stand out against the background, and her gaze, turned upward, meets that of the King on the cross. The other side of the frame, which Christ is turning away from, contains the symbols of the Old Covenant that is coming to an end: the moon, Synagoga, and the torn curtain of the temple. The personification of Death cringes away, in his hand the breaking lance with its point directed at his own head. A branch growing out of the stem of the cross and ending in a demon head causes the bending of Death. The breaking lance illustrates the words of St. Paul: "O death, where is thy victory? O death, where is thy sting?" (I Corinthians 15:55).

Ecclesia appears as a queen with a crown, halo, and chalice, holding the banner in her left hand. Her right hand is raised as she proclaims her tidings, "*Pia Gratia Surgit In Ortum*" (the grace of God rises up like the sun).

Synagoga, opposite her, turns away. She is unstable and drawn into the semicircle of the border, which partly covers her face. Over her shoulder she carries the mantle and roll of the torah and in her right hand the knife of circumcision. At the side are the words, "*Lex Tenet Occasum*" (the law carries the seed of its own destruction). The significance of the composition is summed up in these two banderoles: the way to salvation can be found not in the law of the torah but only in the grace of God. Here, in the generation before the First Crusade, the medieval conflict between Christian and Jew emerged in systematic formulation, even though still contained in the more universal contrast of belief and disbelief, of eternal life and eternal death, which forms the main theme of the composition. The dispute between the queens is merely suggested. Synagoga's "blindness" is indicated by the overlapping frame. Significantly, she stands on the side of death–the wages of sin. The contrast between Christian and Jew is clearly articulated as a contradiction; it is as irreconcilable as life and death. There is no sharing of colors between them, as in the illustration in Drogo's Sacramentary.

This didactic illumination testifies to the integrating tendency of early scholasticism and theology, of symbolism and art. The harmony of the spheres and the relationship of music, grammar, mathematics, and the divine order was explicitly set forth; our theme became wordier; banderoles of doctrines and explanations state their message as determined by church doctrine. Art became more "engaged." The two female figures were only representatives of a doctrine, which, moreover, was distributed over several allegories. They were relieved of their scenic roles and did not act as human beings, but rather as "pure" representatives of an idea, as legible as the writing on the banderoles.

In the Tegernsee missal (Codex 4-VIII.143, Rossiana, Vienna) dating from shortly before the First Crusade, parts of this didactic composition recurred. Here, too, Ecclesia and Synagoga appear only in the medallions along the side; the unrolled torah covers one eye of Synagoga—yet with the other eye she glances back at the cross.

Finally, this illumination in the Uta manuscript was used as late as the fifteenth century as a model for a drawing in the Mettener Codex (Staatsbibliothek, Munich)—proof of the basic significance of those didactics. This late reproduction, originating about four centuries after the Uta manuscript, naturally made considerable use of the changes in the figure of Synagoga that occurred primarily in the twelfth century: here Synagoga is blindfolded and has a goat's head and a Jew's hat (see Chapter 9).

These didactics are also found on church implements, necessarily in shorter form and thus leading to shortcuts and dangerous oversimplifications. On the arms of an ivory cross (Copenhagen) belonging to Gunhild of Denmark (ca. 1075), Ecclesia is related to eternal life and Synagoga to eternal death (Figs. 8 and 9). Whereas Ecclesia is built into the medallion as a static block, the figure of Synagoga is dispersed in diverging lines and covers the whole circle. She is half naked; like the high priest at Christ's interrogation, she has ripped her garment and torn her hair. The reverse side of the cross shows Christ, as judge of the world, between the blessed in Abraham's bosom and the damned in hell. The inscriptions come from Matthew 25:34 and 41: "*Venite Benedicti Patris Mei*" (Come, O blessed of my Father) and "*Dicedite a Me Maledicti in ignem*" (Depart from me, you cursed, into the eternal fire). This judgment was still purely theological. The damned in hell were still only sinners without emblems, merely didactic figures. Not until the era of the crusades were they finally identified with the Jews of the Middle Ages.

The development of the theme prior to the crusades with its growing hostility toward Synagoga will be concluded with a primitive yet expressive ivory tablet from Italy (Fig. 11).[5] The angel directs Ecclesia—who appears in a rich Byzantine costume—to the Lord on the cross. The same angel drives away Synagoga, an old woman who raises her arms in fright. The engraver had portrayed the *unio mystica* as a real event, as suggested in the sermons of St. Augustine (see Chapter 3). While Christ is wedded on the cross to Ecclesia, Synagoga, the mother of Christ who "gave birth to Him in the flesh," is banished from the scene of the wedding. Here, as in the Bargello plate (Fig. 7), sun and moon have changed places.

IV

These pictographic portrayals, created from simplified dogma for didactic purposes, stand in notable contrast to the works of art that challenge the viewer to contemplate a far-reaching religious truth. The contrast Ecclesia-Synagoga was not exaggerated to the point of a contradiction; the iconography of the Carolingian ivory tablets endured; the artistic, and thus the religious, significance of the two women at the foot of the cross remained in equilibrium. Three ivory tablets dating from the early eleventh century (Tongern, Brussels, and Essen) [6] followed the Carolingian tradition. Synagoga again stands opposite Ecclesia at the foot of the cross carrying a hyssop branch, the Old Testament symbol of purification and salvation in the Old Covenant (see Psalm 51, David's prayer of penitence). The contrast of the two allegorical figures was reconciled here under the influence of the *Concordia Veteris et Novi Testamenti*. In the plaque in Tongern (Fig. 12) the chalice scene is also missing. Christ seems united in a mystical, invisible way with Ecclesia whose gaze meets his own. Synagoga also turns her head toward Christ as she departs.

The Brussels tablet (Fig. 13), the model for the one in Essen, adds the story of Christ's birth and ascension to the older iconography and thus becomes a schematic compendium of the life of Christ. Synagoga, carrying the hyssop branch, looks questioningly at John, who stands beside her.

In the ivory tablet in Darmstadt (Fig. 14), which was produced in Cologne in the early eleventh century, the old concept of reconciliation is most clearly portrayed.[7] The classical moderation of the composition corresponds to the idea of equilibrium. Mary on the left and John on the right occupy dominant positions in the foreground, so that the two female figures are half hidden behind them. Ecclesia raises her chalice in a gesture of pure adoration; Synagoga looks up at the crucified Savior, holding her banner erect, without any sign of humiliation. Recalling the formal tradition of antiquity and the ideas of the Carolingian period, the majesty of the retiring queen was preserved in that century ending with the First Crusade. This was the same spirit of *Concordia*, which returned a hundred years later in the sermons of Bernard of Clairvaux and in the *Ludus de Antichristo.*

Chapter 2

Harmony and Discord in God's Redeeming Work

Truth is not silent even in the mouth of its enemies.
—PSEUDO-AUGUSTINE

I

Since Ecclesia and Synagoga symbolically reflected the relationship of the Old Covenant to the New Covenant, the question arises as to the significance of the Old Testament for Christianity in the Middle Ages. Theologically, this relationship was fundamentally established: the Old Testament is the preparatory stage, the essential prerequisite for the New Testament; the Bible is a self-contained unit of creation, revelation, and salvation. The creation of man, the constantly renewed covenant of God with His creation, the messianic prophesies, and the Psalms are harbingers of the act of redemption that finally takes place in Christ's birth, his tidings, his death, and his resurrection.

This concept of the inner unity of the old and the new doctrine, of its temporal and historical succession, could be supported by Jesus's own words. He derived his messianic claim and his concept of God from the traditions of his people. The fusion of the Old and the New Testaments in a greater unity—in the "Entire Holy Scriptures" as it was still being called by Luther—is expressed in numerous passages in the Gospels, but most clearly in the last chapter of the Gospel of Luke: ". . . everything written about me in the law of Moses and the prophets and the psalms must be fulfilled. Then he opened their minds to understand the scriptures . . ." (Luke 24:44 ff.).

It was the unshakable belief of the early Christians that the religious expectation of Judaism had been fulfilled in the life and teachings of Christ. This belief gave force to their words and deeds and produced a historical effect in the conversion of Paul. The basic ideas of the Pauline letters are the overcoming and supersession of the law through God's love as revealed in the life of Christ—the sequence of stages of divine revelation and the union of the old and the new revelations.

The incorporation of the Old and New Testaments into one and the same doctrine of salvation was systematically extended by the early church fathers. An appropriate passage from the writings of Paulinus of Nola (ca. 400) was quoted repeatedly in the following centuries:[1] "The Old Covenant establishes the New, the New fulfills the Old: in the Old is hope, in the New, faith. But Old and New are wedded by the grace of Christ."

The doctrine involved not only the relationship of Judaism to Christianity but also the religious assessment of paganism that became inevitable in the Roman Empire. This is seen in the echo of these issues in the writings of St. Augustine. "In pre-Christian times among other peoples there were also those who, belonging to the spiritual Jerusalem, lived in accordance with God's will and were pleasing to him" (No. 475—*De civitate dei* XVIII, 47). Pious heathendom is the first step in the doctrine of salvation: "That which is now called the Christian religion was also present among the people of ancient times as far back as the beginnings of the human race. It was not absent until Christ's appearance in the flesh, but from then on the true religion that had always been present was known as the Christian religion" (No. 472—*Retractationes* I, 12, 3).[2]

The organic unity and chronological succession of the two Testaments, God's concealment in the Old Covenant and his revelation in the New, was expressed emphatically over and over, though with fine nuances. "It is not correct that everything in the New Testament is presaged in the Old Testament, but it is true that almost everything is. The promise of the kingdom of heaven, for example, is not. However, the two commandments to love God and one's fellow man are there, and the law, the prophets, and all the Gospels and apostolic teachings can be traced back to them" (No. 442–*Retractationes* I, 21, 2). "The Christian Church has grown out of Judaism and heathendom. These two foundation-walls come together from different directions and unite in Christ as the corner pillar." [3]

Any number of such passages can be found in the writings of St. Augustine. What was to be significant for the future was the conceptual pair of obscurity and clarity, of concealment (*velatio*) and revelation (*revelatio*). This pair of reciprocal concepts persisted throughout the religious history of mankind and finally found its historical form in the succession of the Old and the New Covenant: "In the Old Testament, the New is concealed; and in the New Testament, the Old is clarified" (No. 440–*De catechisandis rudibus* 8); and "The righteousness of God by which the believer is led to salvation is concealed in the Old Testament but revealed in the New" (No. 441–*De spiritu et littera* 18). Synagoga and Ecclesia, the veil and the revelation, are the principal representatives of the divine transformation.

In the early Middle Ages this relationship of the two Testaments took shape in a fundamental and significant concept, the *Concordia Veteris et Novi Testamenti.* In this, Judeo-Christian monotheism was reduced to a very simple formula, one which proved practical and viable in missionary work, in sermons, and in liturgy. The fruitfulness of this concept can be traced throughout an entire millennium and is preserved today in outstanding works of art.

The inner harmony of the two Testaments in ideas, events, and figures was proclaimed here. Every event and every doctrine in the New Testament writings already lay dormant like a grain of seed, a prophecy in some passage of the Old Testament, and was now revealed as the fulfillment of a promise made to the forefathers: "*In figuris praesignatur / Cum Isaac immolatur / Agnus Paschae deputatur / Datur manna patribus*" [4] (it is announced in "figures": through Isaac's immolation the paschal lamb is sacrificed and manna bestowed on the fathers). The Old Testament was frequently represented by a mirror or a veil, in keeping with St. Augustine's idea, whereas the divine truth was completely and truly revealed only in the New Testament. At the heart of this exegesis were the prophetic books that almost verse for verse were associated with particular events in the life, death, and resurrection of Christ. This parallelism was eventually extended to all the books of the Bible: thus the association was made between the flight to Egypt and Jacob's flight from his brother; Christ's entrance into Jerusalem and the victorious return of David; Christ's crucifixion and the sacrifice of Isaac or the death of Abel. The event in the Old Testament became a prototype for the event in the New Testament and was understood as a promise of future fulfillment. This typology[5] became a dominant compositional principle in art as the visual revelation of the *Concordia Veteris et Novi Testamenti*. Frescoes, murals, miniatures, and later glass-paintings and sculpture conformed to this principle. The arts owed their intellectual flowering at that time to this typology.

Jewish tradition in the first centuries of the Christian era showed a similar parallelism that, along with the ideas of St. Augustine, probably served as a model for the Christian typology. The Ten Commandments were laid out on two tablets in a way that suggests certain relationships. For example, opposite the words "Thou shalt have no other gods before me" were the words "Thou shalt not commit adultery." Thus the statement is made that whoever worships idols is to be regarded as if, in turning from God, he were being unfaithful to his wife.[6] Here a basic religious experience was expressed: moral doctrine and divine doctrine are inseparable. Jewish and Christian typologies embodied this basic experience throughout the whole course of their diversified histories.

This typology appeared fully developed as early as the fifth century in the wood reliefs on the doors of Santa Sabina in Rome and in the sixth century in the mosaics of San Vitale in Ravenna. Later it appeared in bronze reliefs in Pisa, Monreale, Gnesen, and Verona. An early example in Germany is the bronze door of the cathedral in Hildesheim, dating from about the turn of the millennium. In a descending row on the left, eight scenes from the creation to the murder of Abel tell how man forfeited paradise; in an ascending row on the right, scenes from the annunciation to the resurrection tell the story of how paradise is regained through the sacrifice of Christ's death. Significantly, the fall of man and the crucifixion are depicted opposite each other as "types," as are God's judgment of the first sinners and the judging of God's son by sinful man (represented by Pontius Pilate).

In the succession of figures on the front portal, the typology found its most magnificent form–especially in the rows of prophets and apostles standing opposite one another and dominating the scene and in the significant arrangement of Old and New Testament episodes–finally reaching the crowning union in the scene on the tympanum: the adoration, the crucifixion, the last judgment, and the crowning of Mary. The typology never seems to be static but is constantly permitting new and meaningful relationships and perspectives. It inspires the artistic and religious imagination as well as philosophical speculation. Scholasticism and mysticism enlarged on these ideas, which were then realized in works of art. Thus, the altar of Klosterneuburg in Austria, dating from 1181, presents a polyphonous realization of the typology in fifty-one scenes. The same kind of realization is found later in the Burgundian miniatures (see Chapter 11).

The principle of the *Concordia Veteris et Novi Testamenti* and the typological exegesis derived from it dominated the doctrine and art of the early Christian and medieval periods.[7] The ivory tablets discussed in the first chapter contributed to this exegesis in their own way: the strict and clear symbolism made them members of a higher unity–namely, the *Concordia*. It proved to be so powerful that the typology was even carried through to the narrower framework of the Old Covenant alone: Isidore of Seville found Ecclesia and Synagoga prefigured in the characters of Rachel and Leah: "Leah embraces the figure of Synagoga, who could not perceive God's secrets with the weak eyes of her heart. Rachel, on the other hand, with her clear vision represents the type of Ecclesia–with sharp eyes she comprehended the secrets of God." [8]

The same typology was found in the New Testament: Peter, the first to enter the Lord's tomb on Easter morning, became the type of Ecclesia; and John, who waited for him although he had arrived first at the grave, became the type of Synagoga.[9]

This particular typology, which goes back to Gregory the Great, was without a doubt one of the factors in determining the arrangement of the figures on several ivory tablets where John appears on the right side of the picture in the company of Synagoga (see Figs. 3, 4, and 12–14), forming an artistically and intellectually closed group with her, while Mary remains associated with Ecclesia. John retained this position at the foot of the cross in many medieval representations, long after Synagoga had disappeared from the iconography.

This typological understanding of Ecclesia and Synagoga was free of all conflict, as is most evident in the previous examples; a temporal succession, or a sequence of stages of revelation, is suggested. The two allegories are members of a higher unity. (It can be said here—and we shall return to this later—that the two figures in Bamberg and Strasbourg would also appear again under the influence of *Concordia*, enriched and strengthened by new religious and artistic experiences.) To be sure, symbols of alienation and hostility had also fully developed. They derive from historical claims of authority and sectarian differences. But the oldest root of difference and discord is found in the same soil as the root of *Concordia*, namely, in the wording of the earliest Christian documents. Harmony and discord derived from the same source, the New Testament: harmony insofar as the Testament is doctrine, idea, and revelation; discord insofar as it became history.

II

The system of thought of *Concordia*, which was self-contained as an idea and doctrine of Christian revelation and offered many possibilities for artistic development as a typology, masked and concealed the historical conflict that preceded it. The Gospels are rooted in the religious and prophetic heritage of Jewish monotheism, but the young Christian movement was also nurtured by another source: the contemporary conflict that Jesus had to wage with his Jewish surroundings, the priests in the temples, and the popular, nationalistically inclined messianic expectations. The conflict culminated in the crucifixion but it did not end there. It was continued in the sufferings and persecutions of the Christian sect by the synagogue, of which the Acts of the Apostles and the letters of Paul bear ample witness. The words from the cross "Father, forgive them, for they know not what they do" was Jesus's final answer in the conflict that brought him to his death. In the spirit of the imitation of Christ, this answer resounded in the sufferings of the apostles as the only possibility of winning the conflict.

For an understanding of Ecclesia and Synagoga it is essential to see these conflicting forces, the antagonism betrayed in the New Testament, just as clearly as we see the idea of *Concordia.* Jesus's teachings had grown out of the timeless roots of Jewish monotheism and prophesy; the opposition that he evoked defended itself on the basis of contemporary circumstances, the claims of the law-abiding priesthood, the practice of service in the temple, and ritual. "The Master of all peoples had become the party leader of the lawful, and obedience to the Ruler of history had become an intricate technique of piety" (Dibelius, *Jesus*, p. 35).

Jesus's teachings devalued legal, cultic, and nationalistic views such as those concerning the Sabbath, the observance of fasting, and the Roman head-tax and disappointed the hopes for the establishment of a messianic kingdom on the foundation of the Jewish people. The practice of piety for the Jews relied on the written word, so that everything had to be derived from and proved by the scriptures. Jesus, however, did not derive his message in the last analysis from scripture; he knew the pure will of God from ancient sources of prophetic revelation. The spirit moves where it wills. Jesus repeatedly contrasted "what was told to our forefathers" and "but I say to you." "That could only appear as heresy in the eyes of the Jews. For the voice of the prophets has been silenced and no one has the right to proclaim the will of God on his own" (Dibelius, *Jesus*, p. 108).

The authority that Jesus exercised seemed like blasphemy. The conflict was followed by the passion. But with this death sentence Judaism also passed judgment on itself. "For in the long run it was not to be the campaigns of the Romans that made it homeless, but the hostility of the Christians. Thus the conflict between Jesus and the Jews had fateful consequences" (Dibelius, *Jesus*, p. 106).

Christianity came into being amidst this hostility. Its historical and religious mission could have been the overcoming, in the spirit of its Lord and Savior, of this hostility. The treatment afforded the Jews at the hands of the eventually victorious church and Christian society through the centuries is a touchstone for this mission and its solution.

Concordia, understood as a pure image of divine revelation, had to be concerned only with the intellectual side of the Judeo-Christian tradition. It could overlook the contradictory nature of historical events in which harmony and discord, agreement and opposition, and dominance and rebellion were but constituent parts of the same great historical phenomenon. *Concordia* was an abstraction, a theological definition, an ideal. The Jewish religion had found its place in it, to be sure, but not the surviving representatives of the Jewish religion, who, after the destruction of their capital, were dispersed into minorities living all over the world. Only rarely did *Concordia* offer them refuge. This fact explains (without excusing) why the life of these minorities was so uncertain, so threatened by dangers, persecution, and death. Anyone who is familiar with the history of the Jews in the Middle Ages and compares it with the ideal system of *Concordia*, or anyone who attempts on the basis of this history to establish a connection with the sublime beauty of the figures of Synagoga in Bamberg and Strasbourg, finds himself in a virtually irreconcilable conflict. The dialectical contrast between idea and history, spirit and society, theology and church practice is scarcely clearer than it is here.

The conflict is plainly and ominously formulated in the twenty-third chapter of the Gospel of Matthew in Jesus's sermon reprimanding the scribes and Pharisees. One can hardly believe that Jesus himself spoke this eightfold "Woe to you" (Matthew 23:13–34) in such an irrevocable manner; it was probably the echo of the various similes and aphorisms of Jesus that the writer of the Gospel then combined and interpreted in his own way. Perhaps this chapter was even written after the destruction of Jerusalem, which it prophesies so movingly.

Jesus castigates the need of the high ecclesiastical officials for prestige: they seek public honors and have thereby forfeited the keys to the kingdom of heaven; they are zealots and casuists for whom the observation of ritual is more important than justice, mercy, and faith; they are self-righteous hypocrites who, though they blame their fathers for the death of the prophets of old, will not see that they are guilty of the same fateful blindness. The sermon reaches its climax in the damnation of the Pharisees, "that upon you may come all the righteous blood shed on earth . . ." (Matthew 23:35). But that is not the end. Jesus was deeply moved at the thought of the coming judgment. Until the end he was ready to help his people, whom he loved. In this awful moment of judgment and visions of retribution, he conceived the simile of the hen that gathers her chicks under her wings as the best expression of what he would like to do for his people, "and you would not!" (Matthew 23:37).

Who can read this chapter without the disquieting presentiment of bitter struggles, fateful events, and inescapable consequences? The disobedience to God's commandments and the conflict that the prophets had found themselves exposed to for centuries are very clearly defined (one is reminded of the laments of Jeremiah) but, likewise, the medieval history of the Jews was also prophetically anticipated. Anyone familiar with this history will always be moved by the dreadful precision of this visionary passage, and will not be able to avoid the surmise that the medieval pogroms not only borrowed their words and thoughts from this chapter in Matthew (which can be proved), but that they also sought to find in it their justification. This chapter does seem to place the punishment of the "fools and blind men" in human hands—where it had been previously during the Babylonian captivity, the destruction of Jerusalem, and in the parable of the royal wedding (Matthew 22:2–13), which precedes this sermon. Christians in the Middle Ages repeatedly took the sword of vengeance in hand to punish "the people that crucified the Savior." The Christians heard only the trumpets of judgment in this imposing chapter and arrogated to themselves the position of judge; they did not hear the desperate undertone of pity and forgiveness that gives the sermon its Christian greatness.

III

The conflict between priests and prophets was carried to the historic break in the book of Acts. The internal forces that brought into existence and held together the early congregations were the mystic experience of direct contact with God through visions and revelations, the presence of Christ in the community of the apostles, and the belief in his resurrection and coming again. This depth of feeling was renewed not only by the living memory of Jesus and his spirit, but also by the prophetic writings, and it grew under pressure of external danger. "One must obey God more than men" was St. Peter's last, resolute, and fervent declaration.

The accusation against St. Stephen, the first martyr, was the same as the one against Jesus: he is alleged to have spoken blasphemously of Moses, God, "this holy place" and the law (Acts 6:13). The speech he made in his defense before the high council brings out the contradictions between the worldly and religious history of the Jewish people and the blindness of the Jews to the will of God. Characteristically, it is interrupted at that point where, with reference to the prophet Isaiah, he questions the sacredness of the temple: "Yet the Most High does not dwell in houses made with hands; as the prophet says, 'Heaven is my throne, and earth my footstool. What house will you build for me, says the Lord, or what is the place of my rest? Did not my hand make all these things?' " (Acts 7:48 ff.). St. Stephen was thereby defying not only the power of the priests but the piety of the common people as well. Deeply ashamed of his people, he added his own sermon in reproof of the Pharisees—bitter words that later become a permanent component in the theme of Ecclesia and Synagoga: "You stiff-necked people, uncircumcised in heart and ears, you always resist the Holy Spirit. As your fathers did, so do you. Which of the prophets did not your fathers persecute? And they killed those who announced beforehand the coming of the Righteous One [Jesus] whom you have now betrayed and murdered, you who received the law as delivered by angels and did not keep it" (Acts 7:51–53). But the last words of St.

Stephen did not come from the bitterness of injured love, but were again a prayer of forgiveness for his enemies.

The persuasive power of this depth of feeling, this prophetic certainty, becomes especially clear in two passages in the book of Acts. Gamaliel, a member of the high council, advises his colleagues not to summon "these men" (the apostles) before their tribunals, but to leave it to God to judge them, since they (the scribes) might otherwise find themselves in the dangerous position of "opposing God" (Acts 5:34 ff.). One can watch over or even compel the observance of external formalities, but one cannot judge the sincerity of the inner life. With this, the possibility of prophetic authority was fundamentally conceded.

The second instance is that of Paul, a pupil of Gamaliel, on the road to Damascus. Insofar as we know the life story of Paul, the conflict between a religion of law and a religion of faith filled his entire life. He experienced it and pondered it from both viewpoints—first as a Pharisee and Jew, and then as a Christian. How great the burden of this conflict was and what it demanded of him, he expressed often and movingly (II Corinthians 11:24 ff.). In his person the conflict developed fully and achieved historic significance in his travels. The life and words of Jesus did not lead merely to the imitation of Christ in him, as in the case of St. Stephen but also to a fruitful and continued activity in sermons, letters, and teaching. His letters are among the most valuable treasury of ideas in Christendom: he made the most significant and lasting contribution to the understanding of Jesus's life and mission; he clearly distinguished Christian morality from that of the Jews and heathens; he gave the growing congregations a feeling of both independence and unity; he consciously and consistently drew the line between external obedience to the law and justification by faith; he conceived the idea of a new community of the Holy Ghost, the "church," which encompasses all mankind and in which national, social, and sectarian barriers are removed. "There is neither Jew nor Greek, there is neither slave nor free, there is neither male nor female; for you are all one in Christ Jesus" (Galatians 3:28). "For there is no distinction between Jew and Greek; the same Lord is Lord of all and bestows his riches upon all who call upon him" (Romans 10:12).

The effects that this development was bound to have on Judaism as a people and as a religion can be only vaguely inferred from the book of Acts. The heavy and dogged, often violent, opposition that Paul found among his people, the implacable hostility that brought him before the highest officials of the people and eventually to Rome, is not clarified in the text. Behind this hostility was concealed the question of the continued existence of Judaism as a religion and as a people.[10] Paul broke through the sectarian and national isolation in which the Jews lived, of which they were proud, and in which they served their God; he threatened their religious confidence as the chosen people (something that Jesus had already done and that was present in a germinal stage in the prophets); he promised the heathens salvation by faith without binding them to the law of Moses, and he did it in the name of the same God that the Jews worshipped as God of their fathers. He left to the law only a psychological value, the rank of a transitional stage in which divine truth can be perceived only in veiled form.

This development seemed unavoidable if the idea of a universal God, presaged by the prophets and revived in the prophecies of Jesus, was to achieve historic dimensions. Otherwise this idea would have remained conealed in the isolation of Jewish life. But this development was also tragic, for it split the common foundation and projected the conflict into the centuries to follow. Since the hostility had derived from the natural, inherent conflict of every historical religion between inner feeling and outer form, between prophet and priest, it could be foreseen that not even the new church would be spared this conflict.

Paul saw this danger and combated it "so that salvation may be claimed without proof of the new life," so that there might be a reliance on the forgiveness of sins "even though the abhorrence of sin and the imitation of Christ be missing." Faith and mercy, the experiencing of God in the heart of man and its verification through deeds, would then recede behind a new legalism, a new ritual. And the time could be foreseen when the warning of Gamaliel to the Jewish scribes would appear worthy of being noted by the priests of the New Covenant—specifically, whenever they found themselves confronted with the living conscience that derived its authority and certainty from faith or from mystic depths, a direct knowledge of God independent of formalism.

Chapter 3

Mystical Wedding and Disputation

Righteousness without great humility before God
Becomes at once a dreadful, odious thing.

—MECHTHILD VON MAGDEBURG
(Thirteenth Century)

I

The relationship between Matthew and the lamentations of Jeremiah was mentioned in Chapter 2. Even though they were separated from one another by six centuries, both authors were affected by similar historical events. Both were governed by the same emotions, by the same vision and anger, injured love and pity. Before the mind's eye of the ancient poet and prophet stood the figure of Jerusalem the Queen, the daughter of Zion, dethroned and humiliated, divested of her crown, taken prisoner and derided "for . . . the iniquities of her priests, who shed in the midst of her the blood of the righteous. They wandered, blind, through the streets, so defiled with blood . . ." (Lamentations 4:13–14). In the same way, the fate of the Jewish people took shape again in this figure in the Gospels: "O Jerusalem, Jerusalem, killing the prophets and stoning those who are sent to you!" (Matthew 23:37).

The daughter of Zion, Jerusalem the Queen, survived the destruction of the temple, the end of the kingdom, and the victory of Christianity. Her poetic and symbolic existence outlived the historical event and the nation she represented; she found herself transposed into the liturgy, hymns, and sermons of the Christians. She became a type of Christian doctrine, contrasted with Ecclesia, the church of the New Covenant. Long before the two appeared on the book covers of the Metz school, they were permanent parts of the sermon and liturgy. The lamentations of Jeremiah resounded every year in the Good Friday service: "The crown has fallen from our head; woe to us, for we have sinned! For this our heart has become sick, for these things our eyes have grown dim . . ." (Lamentations 5:16–17), followed by the entreaty "Jerusalem, Jerusalem, turn to thy God."

From here the concept and form of Synagoga developed in the imagination of the early church fathers; she was introduced into the ever-growing fabric of typology as if she were a genuine biblical character. Prudentius's paraphrase of the lamentations goes as follows: "Jerusalem has sinned, therefore she must be like an unclean woman. All who honored her now scorn her because they see her nakedness; but she sighs and has turned away. . . ." Elsewhere it reads: "This voice, O Juda, did not reach thy ears! It did, but it did not penetrate the spirit that is so destitute of light. Thus, banished from the portal she withdrew" (Migne's *Patrologia Latina*, Vol. 60, p. 319). The figure of Synagoga was developed from another passage, that of the return of Moses from Mount Sinai (Exodus 34):

> The leader of the sinful people has returned from the mountain of flashing lightning where God spoke with him; he carries the tablets, carved with trembling fingers, to the tents of the blind. But the people fall on their faces so as not to see the Savior who now has become part of the mystery of the dark law. Wretched woman thou art, who will seek to hide in the dim light with fearful gaze, thy countenance veiled with thy garment! But we comprehend Christ, the veil is lifted from our eyes . . . [Cahier and Martin, *Vitraux peints*, I, 66].

In the hymns of St. Ambrose, whose sermons converted Augustine to Christianity, the same image of the fateful blindness of the Jews appears: "Here, where the words of salvation are proclaimed by all voices, Juda, along with the blind people, rejects the clear path of truth" (Cahier and Martin, *Vitraux peints*, I, 66). And the following quotation from Ambrose may have served as text for one of the ivory tablets from Metz (Fig. 6; see also pp. 6–7). "The blade of circumcision has already become dull, and the sharpness of the stone knife falls into disuse through Jesus. The Christian people are known by their faces, not by their genitals; by baptism, not by a scar. . . ."[1] The following passage comes from Venantius Fortunatus: "Why, Jewish multitude, do you still act unwisely at your age? Learn as an old man to believe, so that you may gain life. Comprehend, white-haired old man! Although robbed of your youth, let greater honor attend your old age. . . ."[2]

This literary figure—Jerusalem, Judea, or Synagoga, a personification of a type, a creature of flesh and blood ready to act and suffer—passed through the centuries that followed. Even in the writings of Bernard of Clairvaux, whose enlightened and tolerant attitude toward the Jews of his time will concern us later, this figure appears in the thousand-year-old, antagonistic meaning: "Isaiah proclaimed it, as Synagoga well knows; yet she will not forsake her blindness. She will not believe her own prophets nor the heathen Sibylline Books—yet it is prophesied! Wretched woman, prepare yourself; believe or abdicate! Why do you wish to be rejected, wretched tribe?" (Cahier and Martin, *Vitraux peints*, I, 66).

In Jeremiah Jerusalem the Queen has God's messengers killed and closes her eyes and ears to the teaching; she is at strife with God and is prone to apostasy; she does not ponder the truth that lies hidden in the prophets. Representations of her reveal gestures of consternation, fear, ignorance, and stubbornness. She is not willing to abdicate and defends her banner, temple, and crown against Ecclesia's grasp. In this respect the eighth- and ninth-century sculptors faithfully followed the wording of the Bible and the hymns (Figs. 5 and 6).

The principal motif was Synagoga's blindness. It went back not only to Matthew 23, to the speech St. Stephen made in his own defense, and to the lamentations, but also to the entire Old Testament, where blindness as a sign of apostasy and of disbelief recurs over and over. We see it in Isaiah's vision (7:9–10) and most powerfully at Mount Sinai: Israel has turned from God and cannot endure the transfiguration in the face of Moses; he has to cover his face with a veil when he steps before the people (Exodus 34:33 ff.). The mystery of God is unbearable to the weak eyes of sinful humanity.

The Christian interpretation of this passage came from Paul: through the teaching and death of Christ he saw this veil torn and God's mystery revealed, but it continues to be hidden from the Jews: ". . . for to this day when they [the Jews] read the old covenant, that same veil remains unlifted . . . but when a man turns to the Lord the veil is removed. . . . And we all, with unveiled face, [behold] the glory of the Lord . . ." (II Corinthians 3:14 ff.).

And finally, it became elevated to a general religious signifiance far above the conflict of the two systems of salvation: "For now we see in a mirror dimly, but then face to face. Now I know in part; then I shall understand fully, even as I have been fully understood" (I Corinthians 13:12).

This symbolism is found in the Gospels as well: God will reveal himself only while he conceals himself. In response to the question of the disciples as to why he spoke in parables, Jesus answered that the truth would shine through the parable for those who knew the secrets of the kingdom of heaven (Matthew 13:11), but that whoever closed his mind would become completely hardened. And in Mark 4:22 ff. it states: "For there is nothing hid, except to be made manifest; nor is anything secret, except to come to light. If any man has ears to hear, let him hear." The train of Christian thought followed this symbol, passing from the veil that covered Moses's face to the curtain of the temple, from the blindness of the daughter of Zion to the parables of Jesus and the letters of Paul, and sought to find therein the secret of the progressive revelation of God. Among the church fathers this set of associations crystallized into concrete dogma and, in the hymns, into poetic images. Later, when Ecclesia and Synagoga appeared in the plastic and graphic arts, and when symbolic and dogmatic speculation reached their high point during the period of the crusades, the veil that was to cover the eyes of Synagoga had long been woven. Blindness as a first stage of revelation is made evident in the portrayal. The symbolic use of the veil, fertile in ideas but frequently obscure, began in the letters to the Corinthians and still affects the viewer today in Bamberg and Strasbourg with tragic force, with love and sympathy, as do the lamentations of Jeremiah and the "Sermon against the Pharisees," which end in a prayer for mercy and a promise.

The blindfold that Synagoga wears would disappear from art along with her. But in its older form as the veil covering Moses's face and as the curtain of the temple, it remained an enduring element in Christian art. The angel of the annunciation, delivering the glad tidings to Mary, draws back the curtain before which Mary is sitting (Schongauer; Dürer, Fig. 17). Here the *revelatio* occurs literally in the surroundings of a middle-class interior. Grünewald portrayed the annunciation between curtains that are already drawn back. The birth of Christ also frequently takes place behind a half-opened curtain. The closed curtain, the first stage of revelation, also found its way into monumental architecture, most impressively on the west portal at Reims.[3]

In the church of St. Martin in Metz there are "two unusual reliefs. . . . The one shows only a closed curtain, as if the birth scene were to be imagined behind it; in the other, the curtain is half drawn back and one sees Mary lifting the newborn child out of the manger." [4] The curtain, forerunner and paraphrase of the veil of Synagoga, was reduced here to its metaphorical components: it is closed and then it is opened, as in the picture, before the eyes of the viewer.

A similar sequence occurs to the veil covering Moses's face: in the window of Suger in the abbey church of St. Denis (see Chapter 9), Moses stands with veiled head while Christ, beside him, lifts the veil. Claus Sluter shows the veil drawn far back on his enormous bust of Moses (Dijon; Fig. 15). Finally, the Moses of Michelangelo (Fig. 16) is unveiled: the divine truth can be seen in his face; we are considered worthy to see clearly the reflection of God in him, as Paul had prophesied. This was the final and decisive paraphrase of the veil of Synagoga, at a time when she herself had already disappeared from art.

II

Synagoga was a creation of prophetic poetry; she was conceived by Jeremiah, recalled to mind in Matthew 23, woven into the typological exegesis of scripture by Paul, and confirmed in this position by the church fathers and hymnists. Ecclesia had a comparable genesis. In her the Christian doctrine of salvation created one of its personifications. The creative idea is found in the letter of Paul to the Ephesians (5:25): "Husbands, love your wives, as Christ loved the church and gave himself up for her, that he might sanctify her. . . . Even so husbands should love their wives as their own bodies. . . . For this reason a man shall leave his father and mother and be joined to his wife, and the two shall become one. This is a great mystery and I take it to mean Christ and the church [Ecclesia]."

The idea that the church was the bride of Christ gained influence from the typology as well: its type was discovered in the Old Testament in the Song of Songs, which even in Jewish exegesis had been understood as an allegory of God's love for the people of Israel. Psalm 45 as well, the wedding song of the just king, contributed to this allegory: "at your right hand stands the queen in gold of Ophir . . . in many-colored robes she is led to the king, with her virgin companions, her escort, in her train. . . ."

The allegorical representation of Hebrew love poetry and its typological use in the *unio mystica* had significant consequences, in the broadest cultural sense, far beyond Ecclesia and Synagoga. When, centuries later, medieval literature and mysticism undertook to extol earthly love as an aspect of divine love and thus to assign to it a valid place in God's plan, it was done with full confidence in the writings of Paul, the Song of Songs, and Psalm 45. This movement reached its climax in Dante and was felt for sometime afterward in art and morality.

The *unio mystica* was closely connected with the blindness and rejection of Synagoga. Augustine had a creative part in this union: in glowing colors he painted the beauty and the glory of the mystical wedding, but at the same time he also showed the necessity of separation from Synagoga. He did this with tremendous effect on the imagination and feelings of posterity. In scenes of dramatic force the allegories come alive, act, and suffer. The following passages are taken from his interpretation of Psalm 45, the above-mentioned wedding song.

Ecclesia is the new bride, Christ the bridegroom. For the flesh is wedded to the word, of which it has been said "they will not be two, but one flesh." . . . Ecclesia has been chosen from all mankind so that the flesh wedded to the word may be the head of the church . . . let the bride jubilate, the beloved of the Lord. . . . Soon you see the son turning against his father. That sword is brought which resists evil; it ushers in another father, another mother. . . . It will be the son against the father, the mother against her daughter. The people who believed the Jews turn against Synagoga . . . like the daughter-in-law against the mother-in-law; the people who had been heathens are now called the daughters-in-law because Christ is the bridegroom, the son of Synagoga. . . . Who then gave birth to the son of God in the flesh? Synagoga. He will leave father and mother. . . . And who is the mother he leaves? The Jewish people, Synagoga. It is to this that the passage refers that asks "Who is my mother and who are my brothers?" What a wedding song! Behold, amidst the songs of joy the bride herself comes forward. For the bridegroom has come . . . he steps forth with her. "The queen stands on your right" [from Psalm 45] but she that stands on your left is no queen, for she is the one to whom is said, "Go forth . . . from me into the eternal fire." But to the one on the right is said, "Come hither, you blessed of my father and inherit the kingdom that has been prepared for you since the beginning of the world. . . ." [5] [See Figs. 7 and 11.]

The following lines come from Sedulius, a young contemporary of St. Augustine: "Then let Synagoga go, darkened in shame; Christ has been wedded to the church in glorious love. . . ." [6]

With this the significant myth of Ecclesia and Synagoga was fully developed; it provided the point of departure for the Carolingian carvers and continued to have an effect through the centuries. We quote from Notker of St. Gallen (eleventh century):

> He, who comes from on high,
> Became enflamed with love for her [Ecclesia],
> Wipes out with his blood
> The birthmark she inherited from the first
>   mother [Eve, type of Ecclesia].
> By the husband's brilliant beam of light,
> Far from the joys of the bride,
> Let Synagoga be driven
> Off into the darkness of the blackest night.

And elsewhere:

> Let the church of Christ sing
> A song to her beloved;
> For her sake God
> Forsook father and mother,
> Clothed himself in our flesh,
> And drove away Synagoga.[7]

During the height of scholasticism in the Middle Ages, the poetic and symbolic force of the *unio mystica* lived on unbroken—for example, in a Corpus Christi sequence of Thomas Aquinas:

> At the new king's table
> The old Passover Feast was destroyed
> By the new;
> The new chases the old from its place,
> Truth drives the shadow away,
> And the light drives away the night.[8]

What St. Augustine had done for the *unio mystica*, the sermons of Leo the Great did for the crucifixion. Although Ecclesia and Synagoga do not appear in his sermons on the passion of Christ, he was nonetheless one of the literary founders of our theme. He raised the scene of the crucifixion to new heights of shared suffering, imagination, and speculation. He transformed his hearers into witnesses of the passion, companions in suffering, and judges when he told of Judas's betrayal, Peter's denial, the bad counsel of the Jews, and Pilate's crime. His sermons also entered into the Carolingian ivory tablets:

For when Christ gave up the ghost all the elements trembled. And since the sun's brilliance was obscured, the day clothed itself in darkness at an unusual hour; the earth, swaying from the mighty jolts, lost its firmness and hard stone burst and split. In the temple the curtain tore and could no longer conceal the secrets of the Old Covenant; graves opened and many saints who had died returned to life in order to strengthen the belief in the resurrection. Heaven and Earth have thus passed their judgment of damnation on you, you Jews. . . . And since you cried "Let his blood come over us and our children" you have received your just reward in the fact that all the believing heathens received what the godless part of your people had forfeited . . . [Sermo 53; Figs. 3–7].

You drew all people to you, O Lord, when the unworthy priests were deprived of the Holy of Holies by the rending of the temple curtain, so that truth would take the place of the prefiguration [*figura*], realization the place of prophecy, and the Gospel the place of the law. "You drew all people to you, O Lord," so that from now on—now that the secret is fulfilled and revealed—all peoples everywhere will worship what was once celebrated in Judea's temple in obscure symbols [*obumbratis significationibus*] . . . [Sermo 59].[9]

III

The literary documents referred to thus far are theological in nature. They developed typologically in the spirit of *Concordia.* The authors remained aware of the original meaning of the words despite occasional deviations. Leo, in speaking of the dreadful fate that the Jews themselves chose, reminded his listeners of Christ's words from the cross: "Father, forgive them, for they know not what they do." He warned his congregation against hatred and vengeance. St. Augustine's rejection of Synagoga "Go away from me, you accursed ones, into the eternal fire" also stood under the authority of the last judgment, not the authority of men.

However, the era of Augustine and Leo also produced two other documents in which the restraining force of *Concordia* and the wealth of typological associations seemed to be denied. They are the *Altercatio Ecclesiae et Synagogae*, the disputation of the two women, and the *Sermo contra Judeos, Paganos et Arianos, de Symbolo.* Both works were attributed to Augustine in the Middle Ages in order to give them the authority of the great church father.

The unknown author of the *Altercatio*[10] seems to have had some knowledge of Augustine's apologetic writings, but his Latin is barbaric and the Augustinian spirit is absent throughout. Various allusions in the text make it likely that the work originated during the period of decline of the Western

Empire, about the time Odoacer took possession of Italy. However, since the effects of this work cannot be detected until the ninth century, it is also possible that it was a product of the late Carolingian epoch or that it only then acquired the form of sharply antagonistic dialogue, perhaps on the basis of older texts. The *Altercatio* does not approach the color, linguistic charm, or depth of Augustine. In its black-and-white portrayal it denies the memory of *Concordia*. The religious evaluation of Synagoga, and the internal continuity of the Old and New Covenants are almost forgotten. For the first time accusations dominate the conversation exclusively—accusations of blindness, obstinacy, and criminality. It seems significant that this work was incorporated, in the ninth century, into the service for Holy Week in several dioceses in the Frankish Empire and that it retained this authoritative position throughout the entire Middle Ages. The spirit and wording of this work seem to reflect a conflict that came to the surface at that time. We know that around the middle of the ninth century, Frankish bishops officially took very stern measures against the Jews. The inclusion of the *Altercatio* in the Easter liturgy took place at the same time. We are evidently dealing here with an intrusion of political and social forces that threatened the originality and truth of the doctrine. It was at this same time that the Carolingian ivory tablets were carved; at the same time the *Altercatio* appeared in the liturgy, Ecclesia and Synagoga appeared in religious miniatures. This connection cannot be overlooked.

In the role of public prosecutor the author presents to the court two women, Ecclesia and Synagoga, whose claims to ownership have to be settled. Synagoga, "once so rich and powerful," now a widow, lays claim to the property and land that Ecclesia possesses "under imperial law." Synagoga is accused of lying, idolatry, and adultery, whereas Ecclesia "by virtue of her chastity and divine law" is alleged to be the rightful ruler of the world. Ecclesia asserts that she alone is entitled to rule after Synagoga's failure: Synagoga had had her merits and had been God's representative; but since she had turned a deaf ear to the prophets, Ecclesia had taken her place and Synagoga now has to serve her. Synagoga refers to the Old Covenant and says she will yield if Ecclesia can justify her claims on that basis. Triumphantly, Ecclesia exclaims, "Here is the Old Covenant, and I will quote from it." Then begins the actual disputation. However, Ecclesia's principal argument is not taken from the Old Testament but from history: the Empire had become Christian and the high public offices were reserved for Christians since the Jews had lost the state of grace. In response to Synagoga's question as to why, then, the sins of the fathers were still being visited upon the children's children, Ecclesia points to the Old Testament precept of retaliation. Certainly Jesus was sent to the Jews, who at that time were still the chosen people, but long ago the prophets had known about the coming disaster and admonished the people to acknowledge the Messiah. Even the unmistakable and precise prophecy of Isaiah "Behold a virgin conceives and will give birth to a son and they will call him Immanuel" had been disregarded by them.

The dispute turns to the ritual of circumcision. In good faith Synagoga refers to the law of Moses; her opponent brings the problem to a head with the sophism that Jewish women would then have to be excluded from grace. And since the circumcised had not recognized the spiritual significance of the ritual and had not circumcised their hearts, the consequence was disfavor, error, and idolatry. Instead of external signs Christians proudly wore the sign of salvation, the cross, on their foreheads, thereby indicating the internal transformation. (The reader will recall such a gesture on the Carolingian ivory tablets; see Fig. 6.) Finally, Ecclesia presents her decisive claim: she is the young queen, the bride of the Lord to whom Synagoga will have to surrender her office. During this presentation Ecclesia shines in the magical light of the Song of Songs, only to fall back into a shallow argument as to why she is the bride of God and the mother of mankind.

Another point of contention concerns the divinity of Christ and his rising after three days; it requires a long series of quotes, taken from the Psalms and the prophets, which Ecclesia advances in favor of this doctrine. Synagoga's obstinacy toward the divine nature in Christ evokes the greatest indignation; Ecclesia angrily calls her "the most hapless, most wretched, and most foolish of all women and a murderess" whose conscience has been wiped out by crime and error. This argument dominates the last chapter until Synagoga bows to the overwhelming evidence in favor of Ecclesia. The end of the dispute comes unexpectedly; the judges pass no judgment, but the outcome is certain.

An additional scene is found in other versions of the *Altercatio*: Synagoga appears shaken by the remembrance of her crimes against the prophets; woven into the scene is the old prophecy that the Jews also will recognize the Messiah on the day of judgment.

Chapter 4

From Allegory to Figure

Art: another form of nature,
also mysterious, but more comprehensible.
—GOETHE

I

The poor Latin, fragmentary form, and expedient sophistry characterize the *Altercatio* as a product of its time. The historian who searches beneath the layer of the contemporary findings discovers the apologetic treatise as it had been developed on a much higher level, during the patristic epoch. The original apology dealt with the religious aspects of Christian doctrine, the concept of salvation, and the idea of God. The main points were the divine nature of Christ, his messiahship, and the transformation of a ritualistic religion into a purely spiritual one.

Traces of these basic ideas are found in the *Altercatio*. But the *Concordia* was sacrificed, the equilibrium lost, and the judgment pronounced before the dialogue begins. Compared with the religious core these factors were of political and social origin; these external intrusions destroyed the autonomy of the religious aspect and transformed the original truth into a tool of power. Was the Synagoga who appears here still the type of the New Testament, still the essential preparatory stage of revelation, or was she already the distorted image of the Jewish people in a Europe that had become Christian?

Without a doubt the disputation between Ecclesia and Synagoga, the transferring of office and title on three of the Carolingian ivory tablets (Figs. 5 and 6), was suggested by the pseudo-Augustinian *Altercatio*—was indeed determined by it in detail. The disputation on the three ivory tablets and the *Altercatio* derived from the same historical situation, which we shall take up in Agobard's letters (Chapter 6). But even when the dialogue of the disputation appeared so vividly on the ivories as to seem almost audible, the ivories were nevertheless far removed from the spirit of the *Altercatio*, for the dialogue remained incorporated in the wider context of the Christian history of salvation. The proximity of the crucified Christ ensured dignity and equilibrium. In the cosmic drama of salvation the dialogue was only one aspect among many. The *Altercatio*, however, singles out this aspect, isolates it, and turns it into a polemical tract—a clear sign that in this case, we are dealing less with a religious document than with a political one.

But beneath the dubious mediocrity of the *Altercatio* other things lie buried: here, in a way, is the germ of the medieval mystery play, which did not come to life until much later.

Seventy years ago Weber, in his pioneering work on Ecclesia and Synagoga in pictorial art,[1] came to the conclusion that medieval drama had developed in the ninth century from dialogue similar to that in the *Altercatio*, and that scenes presented by clerics in the church had influenced the composition of the Carolingian ivories. This conclusion was untenable; the points of contact of liturgy, drama, and pictorial art still present many open questions.

However, it is obvious that dialogue and confrontation are indispensable elements in the drama; and it was precisely these elements that determine the form of the *Altercatio*, despite learned pretensions and expedient allegories. The way had been prepared for the transformation of abstract ideas into human characters and personal destinies in the hymns and sermons of the church fathers; in the *Altercatio* it was carried even further. In order to be convincing, the concept needed human form, a face, gestures, speech, action. With disputation and action even the *Altercatio* moved toward a high point of dramatic expression that was still far beyond the historical horizon.

When the unknown author of the *Altercatio* endowed his types with virtues and vices of human life—more fully and consistently than the hymnists had done—he opened for them the way that finally led to great art. This transformation was more significant and of greater consequence for Synagoga than for Ecclesia. The former's transformation into a living and suffering creature coincided with the growing conflict between Christian society and the Jewish minorities. The conflict deprived Synagoga of the protection of *Concordia* and forced her onto the level of contemporary history, where she was subjected to the fate of medieval Jewry. The future direction was determined by the *Altercatio*. The accusations voiced here were raised incessantly against the Jews as well as Synagoga in the centuries to come. But her suffering was rewarded when, in the thirteenth century, her picture was placed beside Ecclesia again on an equal status, and she was endowed with such a consummate expression of human life and suffering that we view her with more sympathy than we do Ecclesia in her regal dignity.

II

Much that was said about the *Altercatio* is also true of the *Sermo contra Judeos, Paganos et Arianos, de Symbolo*.[2] This latter work had also been ascribed to Augustine and employs the framework of a court hearing: through the testimony of witnesses the truth about Christ is to be established in the presence of the Jews, who deny this truth. This work found an authoritative position in the liturgy for Christmas week. The part dealing with the Jews contains a list of Old Testament messianic prophecies as they were understood by the medieval church, but in dramatic form; even today one reads this section with intense interest. The direct influence of the *Sermo* on medieval drama is evident, even though the date of its origin is disputed. The *Sermo* developed into the *Ordo Prophetarum*, the prophet play.

The chronological proximity and essential relationship of the *Sermo* and the *Altercatio* justify an examination of the former. The author of the *Sermo* summoned the Jews before a tribunal in order to ascertain why they deny that Jesus is God's son:

Is it not written in your law that the testimony of two men is true? O, you transgressors of the law, pay heed to your own law! If you seek testimony concerning Christ, it is written in your own law that the testimony of two men is true; therefore, let not just two but many witnesses of Christ step forth from your own scriptures and let them shame those who, though hearers of the word, are not doers of the word.

Thus the *Sermo* developed; one prophet after another is asked to testify and quotes from his own writings:

"Now Isaiah, state your testimony concerning Christ."

"*Behold, a virgin will conceive and give birth to a son whom you shall call Immanuel, that is, God with us.*"

"Now let another witness come forward. You, Jeremiah, give your testimony concerning Christ."

"*This is our God and there is no other beside him. He knew all the paths of wisdom and instructed Jacob, His servant, and Israel, His beloved people. Later he appeared on earth and traveled about, speaking with men.*"

"Behold here two witnesses from your own book of laws . . . but let other witnesses come forward . . . let saintly Daniel approach. . . ."

The public interrogation continues in this fashion. Moses, David, Habakkuk, Jeremiah, and Simeon give their testimonies, as do Zachariah and Elizabeth, the parents of John the Baptist.

Finally John himself appears:

"*Who do you believe I am? I am not the one. But know that one will come after me whose shoelaces I am not worthy to unloose. . . . Do you come to me to be baptized? I am in need of being baptized by you. . . .*"

After calling upon these numerous witnesses from the sacred books of the Jews, the *Sermo* quotes from the book of the heathens: "Let us also show that even heathendom bears witness to Christ; the truth has not concealed itself—it is not silent even in the mouth of its enemies. . . ."

Among the prominent heathens who are summoned forth are Vergil, Nebuchadnezzar, and the Sibyl of Cumae. Vergil speaks his prophetic words from the fourth eclogue: "Soon a new lineage shall be sent from heaven on high"; the Babylonian ruler relates his experience with the three men in the fiery furnace; the sibyl quotes her prophecy concerning the coming of Christ, the end of the world, and the trumpets of judgment.

Finally, the author turns again to the Jews: "In the face of this overwhelming evidence do you still dare to defy the truth. . . ."

The purpose of the *Sermo* clearly lay outside the *Concordia*; it reflected the endeavors to convert medieval Jewry. The *Ordo Prophetarum*, which originated in the *Sermo* and later developed into the prophet play, quite openly served the purposes of conversion. At that time, Ecclesia and Synagoga still had no part in the prophet play—the Jews to whom it addressed itself were the medieval Jews, not Synagoga. But the two themes—the apologetic nature of the disputation and the attempts at conversion of the *Sermo*—attracted one another, and the meeting would take place.

Chapter 5

Christians and Jews in the Middle Ages

Our Father, *a splendid prayer,*
It serves and helps in all dismay.
If someone prays the Pater Noster,
In the name of heaven, let him pray.
—GOETHE

I

We will not be concerned here with the history of the Jews in the Middle Ages, but with a historical analysis of the position and acceptance of the system of religious thought to which Ecclesia and Synagoga belong. For this purpose, the first millennium of Christian history proves especially fruitful. Social conditions and legal maxims, political and economic principles influenced the system of religious thought, thus contributing to the development of Ecclesia and Synagoga as indicators of internal peace or internal conflict. The principles that made possible a coexistence of the two religions and the forces that endangered it were already clearly developed in the early Middle Ages, but they somewhat counterbalanced each other, so that the life of the Jewish minorities remained relatively stable.

The late Middle Ages, from approximately the year 1000 on, was characterized by the growing claims of ecclesiastical power over secular power and by the development of the economic system and the class structure. Essentially this period brought only repetition, although in a constantly intensifying form because of the fateful involvement of the Jews in the crises of the early capitalistic epoch. Their destiny as wanderers, their homelessness, their knowledge of languages, and their social isolation had, ever since ancient times, thrust the business professions upon them.

We can hardly go into detail on the economic and historical situation. Theory and practice were contradictory. On the one hand, the doctrine of the "just price" developed, which set ethical limits on prices (developed primarily by Thomas Aquinas). On the other hand, the practice of usury developed; it came out of the Mediterranean countries, gained a foothold in Italy, southern France, Flanders, and the Hanseatic cities and was engaged in by Christians and Jews alike. A middle course between the two principles could not be found, partly because there was still no science of economics but also because the church officially declared the charging of interest in any form to be sinful. It thereby put itself in a precarious and ambiguous situation, since the greatest concentration of money in Europe was soon gathered at the papal court. Furthermore, the practice, which had become common, of selling high ecclesiastical offices would not have been possible without a credit system that extended to all Christian countries.

Although the church itself did not have to come to terms with the consequences of this double standard of morality until the Reformation era, the Jews increasingly became the victims of this duplicity from the eleventh century on. Their unique position—they were exempt from the church's prohibition against charging interest—was strengthened by the growing need for money and enabled them to collect riches and gain influence. This combination of the Jews' special religious position and their unique economic situation soon proved disastrous, however, for their wealth was confiscated on all kinds of pretexts by the king, the princes, and the cities (as "protectors" of the Jews), so that they became "the most convenient objects of taxation." Or, even worse, the "protection" failed completely and abandoned the Jews to the fury of the mob, who avenged themselves on the visible representatives of the monetary economy and seized the opportunity to plunder.

These developments were suggested at the very outset of the crusades, which certainly could not have gotten underway without a credit system and which are part of economic as well as religious history. The union of religious and economic elements brought a decisive change in conditions for the Jewish minorities; the era of the crusades is characterized by many acts of violence against them. Naked force destroyed the kernel of communality in the two religions, and the loss could not be retrieved.

The third phase brought a profound legal and social isolation of the Jews from their Christian surroundings, which finally led, via the ghetto, to complete alienation and lack of understanding on the part of both. Here, too, details will only be discussed when they have a direct bearing on the theme of Ecclesia and Synagoga.

II

The monotheism of Old Testament teaching and the intense feeling of the chosen people had clearly made the Jews of the Diaspora stand out above the contemporary religions. No other religion made such absolute demands. The Diaspora strengthened the social isolation of the Jews, in keeping with their teachings; but it also strengthened the intensity of their religious feeling and zeal for proselytizing. These characteristics evoked hostility as well as admiration; they explain the isolation and unpopularity of the Jews in the Roman Empire, which is often revealed by the authors of antiquity.

Christianity took from biblical tradition not only the belief in the one, benevolent, and almighty God, but also that intensity inherent in minorities and a fervent sectarian zeal for converts. To the casual observer the Christians were little different from the Jews; nor did the persecutors of the Christians make any distinction. But the Christians' unbending and intolerant zeal inevitably collided with the same qualities of the Jews. The discord sown in the Testaments and the variety and capability for development of religious experience and practice were projected into the following centuries.[1] This was intensified by the fact that Christianity was elevated to the dominant religion and the Roman Empire officially became Christian. The civil war within biblical monotheism thereby became permanent. The positions of power had been completely reversed since the initial situation, as described in the book of Acts. Just as the high council of the Jews had been at one time, the church was now in a position to use force: a lasting, permanent temptation for the one in power. On the other hand, it must be stressed that the never-diminishing, creative religious power of Old and New Testament biblical tradition could only be experienced and developed in this contrast of power and spirit, as is shown in the idea of *Concordia.* Only in conflict with the prevailing power could the depth of the revelation be illumined and experienced anew, and the claims of conscience above and beyond form and dogma be asserted. Jews, Christians, and heathens contributed to this in like manner.

In the year 313, when Constantine determined on the historical future of Christianity, the people in the empire—some through compulsion, some indifferently, and others willingly—converted to the new faith. They brought with them the inherited hatred and hostility of the Romans toward the Jews, which further intensified the conflict between Jews and Christians. Constantine forbade the Jews to have Christian servants and thereby, as a Christian authority, endorsed the Jews' self-imposed isolation. Bishop Ambrose of Milan praised the destruction of a Roman synagogue by a mob as an act pleasing to God, and he called Emperor Maximus a Jew because the latter brought about the restoration of the building. Bishop Hilary of Poitiers refused to eat with Jews or to respond to their greeting—an attitude that was later endorsed by church law.

The Code of Emperor Theodosius II, which was enacted in the year 438, clearly reflects this attitude. This law excluded Jews from all public offices and for the first time forbade mixed marriages or the construction of new synagogues. Almost all measures and regulations that were applied more or less systematically in later centuries are found first in the Theodosian Code. Justinian's *Corpus Juris Civilis*, which came into being about the middle of the sixth century, adopted all these principles.

The disintegration of the Roman Empire into various Germanic kingdoms brought decisive changes. A sort of tolerance developed, partly due without doubt to indifference and ignorance, but partly, too, because of the fact that the conquering Teutons were adherents of Arianism, a doctrine that had been regarded as heresy since the time of the Nicene Council (A.D. 325) and one that denied the divinity of Jesus. In this they came closer to the Jewish view, though unintentionally.

In the figure of Theodoric the Great, King of the Ostrogoths (474–526), this Arian view was combined with outstanding statesmanship. He repeatedly defended the rights of Roman Jews against the curtailments imposed by the local clergy. In a document still preserved today, he gave the Jews of Genoa the authority to restore their synagogue. This document ends with the following words: "Why do you strive for a thing from which you should turn away? But we give you our permission, even though we must properly disapprove of this request on the part of heretics; we cannot enjoin a religion on you, because no one can be forced to believe against his will." [2]

This principle, related to the idea of *Concordia*, did not remain in force for long. We find the first forcible conversions of Jews at the end of the sixth century in the Frankish Empire of the Merovingians and in the Spain of the Visigoths. The bishops united against the king and prevailed upon him to present the Spanish Jews with the alternatives of conversion or emigration. Many chose to accept baptism; to prevent backsliding, violent measures were introduced. A situation developed similar to the one which later gave rise to the Inquisition.

This policy ran contrary to the convictions of many clerics, among them Pope Gregory I and Isidore of Seville. The latter's treatise *De fide Catholica ex Veteri et Novo Testamento contra Judeos* was the first systematic portrayal of the religious conflict in the Middle Ages and derived from the spirit of *Concordia*. Isidore of Seville wrote in order to defend his belief and to convert the Jews through understanding and logic, not by repressive measures or force. The sum total of the material he brought together and the nobility of his thoughts made a deep impression on the Middle Ages and continued to have an effect on later writers, although some of them used his arguments to arrive at the opposite conclusions. Even before he died at an advanced age, Isidore witnessed judgments that, as

Döllinger notes,[3] caused more bloodshed and tears than any judgment in heathen antiquity, for they set the pattern for innumerable acts of violence in later centuries. Only the Moslem invasion, which began in 711, restored freedom to the Spanish Jews. With this freedom they produced scientific and philosophical contributions of the highest order, which later, at the proper time, influenced the Christian West.

The opposition to forced conversions was strengthened with the increasing importance of the popes. Gregory the Great, who was pope from 590 to 604 and a contemporary of Isidore, advocated—as did Isidore—the principle that Jews should be converted only by kindness and persuasion. To fanatical bishops and rulers who viewed proselytizing as an activity pleasing to God or who pursued it for political reasons, Gregory preached the principle of tolerance. His pastoral letters contain earnest admonishments such as the following: "We forbid harassment of or discrimination against the Jews . . . ; we permit them to live as Roman citizens and to do as they please with their goods and property; we forbid them only to keep Christian slaves." He repeatedly demanded of Frankish kings that they recognize the Jews and compensate Jewish communities for losses inflicted upon them, without losing sight of the ultimate goal of converting the Jews to Christianity.

Thus, Pope Gregory offered economic advantages to converted Jews as a means of persuasion and in the hope of "at least winning over their children thereby." This was the only external measure that he considered permissible. It appears certain that the church managed to deal with the Jewish question during his pontificate without the aid of hunger, misery, or the ravages of war.

The forced conversions in the Merovingian Frankish Empire toward the end of the sixth century had been preceded by a long period of tolerance. The strict regime of Clovis (481–511) had not yielded to ecclesiastical influences in this regard. At that time the Jews were active not only in business but also in handicrafts and agriculture. We know of Jewish doctors and soldiers, of social intercourse, and even of mixed marriages between Jews and Christians. The synods of the Frankish church repeatedly condemned these conditions. But only after the middle of the sixth century did these synods gain power, and they did so to the extent that the king's power declined. Finally, mixed marriages were forbidden, and the pressure on the Jews to convert intensified.

We possess a significant document from this period of transition. At the time of the attempted conversions directed by Avitus, the Bishop of Clermont, there lived a Jew by the name of Priscus, who had steadfastly resisted all attempts at conversion. He was a business agent of King Chilperic I of Neustria (561–584), who introduced him to the learned Bishop Gregory of Tours, the historian of the Franks, hoping that the Jew would be converted by the intelligence and eloquence of the bishop. A dispute arose between the bishop and the Jew, who was just as well versed in his sacred scriptures as Gregory was in his. The course of this dispute, as recorded by Gregory himself, is of great value[4] since the positions are clearly developed in his document and in no way obscured by external interference.

There are numerous apologetic treatises in the form of disputations in which the equality of the partners is only feigned. These played before the eyes of later generations, for whom the outcome was clear from the start—something that made these disputations so popular. In Gregory's document, however, the interest and presence of the king assured a dispute between two parties that were still equal. The disputed, contradictory basic concepts were presented frankly and with full clarity. The same principles can still be found in the distortions of the *Altercatio*, in the symbolic camouflage of the scholastics, and even in the hatred and contempt that dominate the mystery plays of the fifteenth century. The Jew cannot accept the Christian idea of God, the concept of salvation, and the divinity of Jesus: "God does not need to have the work of salvation performed by a son born in the flesh. He cannot share his divinity with anyone, for there is only one God and this God cannot be beaten, humbled, and crucified." The strict, unyielding Jewish monotheism is clearly developed and, as he himself admitted, Gregory did not succeed in refuting the view of his equally learned opponent. The real conflict is formulated better in this document than anywhere in the Gospels or Acts.

III

With the rise of the Carolingians in France—first as "mayors of the palace" and then from 751 on as kings—a strong central authority was established. Because of this central authority, the position of the Jews improved. The reign of Charlemagne (768–814) was the stage immediately prior to that of the ivory tablets of the Metz school.

Even as the powerful patron of the church, Charlemagne remained free of clerical bias in contrast to Pope Hadrian, who maintained a doctrinaire attitude with regard to the Jews and used his influence in Spain, for example, to isolate the Jews socially and religiously from Christians and Arabs. Charlemagne, however, pursued a course that endangered neither the decrees of the Frankish synods and church law nor political interests. He thereby made use of the trade connections that the Jews maintained with the Mediterranean countries and Asia Minor in order to link, with their help, the Frankish Empire to "world" commerce. In their business activities the Jews were subject only to the same restrictions that were imposed on all merchants. In keeping with this pragmatic political assessment of Judaism is the report that the emperor was interested in the erudition of Jewish rabbis and asked Harun-al-Rashid to send him trained rabbis from the Orient to take charge of education in the Jewish communities of France and Germany.

Under such conditions, the Jews in the West moved into the eastern provinces of the Carolingian Empire—a migration that continued in the following century, into Bohemia and the Slavic lands beyond the Elbe river. Many of these Jews were educated merchants with a command of several languages.

The position of this minority improved further under Louis the Pious. He probably originated the concept of the king as patron of the Jews in the realm. The law to this effect is not preserved, but we know of safe-conduct letters for individual Jews. The holders of such safe-conduct letters could move freely from place to place in their work, acquire property, and have Christians as business partners or employees.

These safe-conduct letters made their possessors direct subjects and protégés of the king without regard to local jurisdiction. In return, they were required to pay high taxes and "serve the king faithfully." We know that a man by the name of Everard was put in charge of Jewish affairs, evidently in connection with the issuing of safe-conduct letters. Owing to their business skill, some Jews were even employed as tax collectors, whereby a degree of authority over Christians devolved on them. This was, of course, in conflict with the teachings and laws of the Frankish church as they had been laid down as long as 300 years previously.

The role of patron of minorities derived from a high and noble concept of regal power. It was the legacy of Charlemagne, and Louis I advocated it despite his acquiescence to the ideas of the clergy in other matters. This legacy, however, finally became too burdensome for him, as is evident in the collapse of his authority and the wars he had to wage against his sons. In general, Louis was determined to maintain the legal standing of the Jews that his father had established. Later developments justified his position. The concept of the Jews as the "Chamberlains of the King" seems to refer to the author of the Carolingian safe-conduct letters.

Economic considerations were a principal reason for the favoritism granted the Jews in the Carolingian Empire. In a yet undeveloped national economy, they made possible an extensive exchange of goods and an orderly monetary system. Like most historical phenomena, this situation was more complex than presented here. In addition, it was rooted in intellectual conditions that developed under the inspiring leadership of Charlemagne during the Carolingian Renaissance. Charlemagne's inquiring and open mind, his thirst for pure knowledge, and his untiring interest in the intellectual life led to a revival of the study of ancient languages, science, and literature and stimulated interest in history and philosophy. With practical foresight he transmitted these interests widely to government officials and the clergy. Characteristically, he returned important state functions—the courts and the administration—to the basis of written documents, decrees, and laws rather than a dependence on oral transmission, as was customary before and after his reign.

Although many clerics played a leading role in these efforts, the entire movement revealed an orientation toward a general education on a secular basis. Likewise, the law of the land was above canon law: the head of the theocratic structure was the emperor, whereas the pope was only the first bishop of the empire. Brilliant and outstanding intellects from all over Europe came together at the court of Charlemagne and his successor: the Franks Angilbert and Einhard, Paul the Deacon (the historian of the Lombards), the Italians Peter of Pisa and Paul of Aquileia, the Visigoth Theodulf, the architect Odo of Metz, and above all the Anglo-Saxon Alcuin, to whose pedagogical genius Rabanus Maurus and Walafrid Strabo owed their learning. History, literature, and theological and philosophical speculation flourished. Finally, the century found its most significant representative in John Scotus Erigena from the Celtic north, who was Alcuin's successor. This brilliant intellectual atmosphere reflected the universality both of the empire and of knowledge.

This universal enlightenment and appreciation for the intellect was bound to ease the burdens of the Jews as well. In some outstanding figures of that time the venerable *Concordia* can again be discerned—that concept in which the spiritual and historical truth of the two rival religions had hitherto found its purest expression. Characteristically, Isidore of Seville's treatise *De Fide Catholica ex Veteri et Novo Testamento contra Judaeos* was translated at just that time into Old High German, the language spoken at the court of the emperor.

Rabanus Maurus, Bishop of Fulda, educator and scholar, and finally Archbishop of Mainz, confessed in his Bible commentary that he had obtained scholarly information regarding Jewish traditions from a learned rabbi. Rabanus dedicated his translation and exegesis of the books of Esther and Judith to Louis's second wife, the empress Judith, in whom the education, manifold interests, and brilliant intellect of the Carolingian Renaissance were more manifest than in Louis.

Rabanus stated that he had translated these books "in the figurative sense"; he praised the two Hebrew women, of whom "one is a queen like yourself and the other bears your name"; he described them as holy, divinely inspired characters and calls them types of the Christian church and forerunners of

God's ultimate triumph. The empress Judith was thus linked with her Hebrew namesake–the one a forerunner, the other an adherent of the Christian doctrine.

Under Charlemagne's rule, the Jews not only had the right to observe, unmolested, their religious practices, but also the right to speak freely about their religion and its principles in the company of Christians. Rabanus alluded to the fact that certain highly educated people "preferred the works of Josephus and Philo to even the Holy Scriptures." Objective religious discussions between Jews and Christians were evidently possible.[5] On such occasions, the Jewish religion may well have been able to develop a persuasive power precisely because it was not burdened with political compromises and abuses as was the dominant Christianity. It may have been to the advantage of Judaism that it played the part of a tolerated opposition without any political responsibility of its own. We read of the conversion to the Jewish faith of Bodo, the emperor's father confessor. He even took this step in Rome, the center of a religion that had become political. This seems to demonstrate the attraction of a belief that consisted only of Old Testament rabbinical tradition and religious service in the synagogue. However, Rabanus, who reported this episode, did not disclose to us the causes.[6]

All in all, it is certain that the *Concordia* was still very much a living concept in Carolingian times and that its practical consequences were recognized and accepted. One of these consequences was the respect in which the Jews were held as "the descendants of the patriarchs and prophets."

Chapter 6

Agobard's Letters

Justice exists absolutely for each person as such,
or it does not exist at all.[1]

—ROMANO GUARDINI

I

While the system of thought of *Concordia* was developing in the Carolingian era, opposing forces were also increasing. For the first time it becomes possible to observe the origin and importance of these forces in the context of their time. The tolerance had derived from deeper religious sources and from the philosophical and historical sincerity of educated laymen. The opposing reaction, on the other hand, had its roots in Frankish church law, which originated in the late Roman era, and found its spokesman in Archbishop Agobard of Lyon. Agobard, too, was indebted to the Carolingian Renaissance. With the thoroughness of the scholar, he had opposed superstition and magic in his writings, as well as ordeal by duel and weather magic. On the other hand, as a high ecclesiastical official he struggled fervently for the priority of ecclesiastical authority over the state and society. "Whoever acts against the church commits a sin against God" was his maxim, which made him a forerunner of the later claims made by the popes to authority over secular rulers.

After the death of Charlemagne, the Frankish clergy became aware of its growing influence and soon felt powerful enough to begin the struggle for restitution of church property that had been secularized for war purposes at the time of Charles Martel. Agobard advocated this claim and did not abandon it even during the rebellion of Louis's sons against their father. When the latter's second wife, Judith, tried to change the right of succession to the throne—which had been arranged with the help of the church—in favor of her own son, Agobard sided with Lothair, Louis's eldest son. The discord within the dynasty led to civil war and finally to the complete collapse of the central authority. Church dignitaries gave their blessing to the revolt of the sons against their father, hoping that the church faction would benefit from the humiliation of the emperor. The backbone of the waning central authority was not the emperor, but Judith; the church faction directed its attack principally against her and her followers at the court. Every means was employed in the struggle; Agobard did not even refrain from personal slander. He approved the action of Louis's sons in deposing their father and was one of the bishops who forced the emperor into the humiliating Atonement of Soissons. In the year 835 Louis was again officially recognized as emperor and Agobard was banished for a time from his archbishopric. Apparently, he finally became reconciled with Louis before both men died in the year 840.

One must bear in mind Agobard's part in this factional struggle in order to understand his harsh statements against toleration of the Jews in private and public life. Five letters,[2] which were written by him between 822 and 828, represent an early phase of his resistance to the central authority.

In the first letter Agobard addressed the high officials of the court, among them members of the imperial family. He put before them a problem that had often been discussed since the time of Constantine:

What shall we do with the heathen slaves that the Jews have bought and are holding in their homes? These slaves learn our language, hear about our religion, are impressed by the solemnity of our divine service; their souls are disposed toward Christian love; they would like to become members of the church; they seek refuge in the church and ask to be baptized. We must either deny them this, or grant it. . . . I maintain that man is in truth the creature of God and that everyone, even a slave, belongs to God. Although a slave owes the work of his body to his earthly master, he must remain true in spirit to his Creator. . . . The apostles did not need the permission of the slave holders in order to baptize slaves . . . ; quite the contrary—they received everyone into the same community and taught them that they were brothers and children of God. . . .

II

Agobard then appealed to the ruler's Christian conscience to permit such slaves to be baptized if they so desired.

We do not propose this in order to deprive the Jews of what they have invested in the slaves; we offer them compensation as provided in ancient statutes; but the Jews do not accept that, in the belief that the government will protect them. . . . Now if we should refuse baptism to Jews and slaves despite their requests, then God will condemn us; if we grant the request, however, I fear that insult and injury will follow for the church. . . .

If no more than this first letter of Agobard were handed down, it alone could document the basic and unavoidable conflict between the conscience of a priest and the prevailing laws. The language is restrained and dignified; no prejudices are disclosed; the safe-conduct letters are not mentioned, although Agobard seemed to be alluding to them when he stated that equality before God must be the only principle when a slave or a Jew requests baptism. Equality before God is a purely religious principle and, at the time of the apostles, had no direct social consequences. Agobard did not yet invoke the older rules of the church that prescribed the redemption of Christian slaves by purchasing them from the Jews; he sought only a tentative basis on which to decide such cases.

In the second letter the problem develops sharper contrasts. Agobard deplored the "godless" law forbidding the baptism of slaves held by Jews and demanded respect for the sacred canon law. Evidently, the baptism of such slaves had become more common, so that the Jews invoked their safe-conduct letters, which explicitly made the baptism of slaves contingent upon the consent of their masters. It is possible that a wave of such conversions had induced the emperor to issue these letters in the first place so that the clergy could not exploit the one-sided situation. The astonishing thing in Agobard's second letter is that he questioned the authenticity of the safe-conduct letters presented to him by the Jews of Lyon and asserted that it was impossible for the emperor in his wisdom to have been so rash. This tactical insinuation by a high dignitary of the empire and of the church seems symptomatic of the growing distrust that later broke into open conflict between the court factions.

The major portion of the second letter consists of biblical passages. These were cited with the intention of proving that the preaching of the gospel at the time of the apostles knew no social bounds but addressed itself instead to all mankind so that a community would come into being: "Here there cannot be Greek and Jew, circumcised and uncircumcised, barbarian, Scythian, slave, free man, but Christ is all, and in all" (Colossians 3:11).

Above and beyond this, however, the letter is full of growing animosity. Agobard was pressing for a test of strength. The measured language of the first letter acquires a demagogic tone in the second: ". . . this matter must not be left to the whim of godless people, who in their falseness not only keep all who live among them away from the teaching of Christ, but also continually curse and offend the believers privately and publicly."

The church itself, Agobard alleged, is endangered by the attitude of the court and Everard's activities.

> This situation troubles not just us, but even more those who could so easily be won for Christ no matter what stood in the way . . . ; the souls which could augment the flock of the shepherd, and for whose salvation we beseech God during Holy Week in every church, remain trapped in the snares of the devil because of the stubborn resistance of those who deny God and who are even abetted in this by the emperor's safe-conduct letters. . . .

In his zeal, Agobard combined new historical views with the religious principles. He had proved the right of even a slave to divine salvation. But in the second letter this Christian principle is identified with canon law as it had been developed in the history of the church. It cannot be verified from scripture that a Jew may not keep Christians as slaves or employ them for pay. The conflict of conscience, which Agobard described so emphatically, is in truth a political controversy enflamed by the distribution of power and property. It had thus become removed from religious principles and its outcome was decided on the basis of power politics. The safe-conduct letters naturally afforded the court a good income, but the countermove of Agobard was also only pseudoreligious in character. The letter presages the conflict, which was soon to erupt, between the clergy and the court. As had happened so often before—and would again later—a religious problem had become a pretext and a means in the struggle for power.

In apparent connection with the second letter, which was addressed to the emperor's counselors, Agobard turned to Louis himself in two later letters, in order to call his attention to a matter that, in Agobard's opinion, was being poorly managed. The third letter is a personal appeal to the conscience of the emperor and a complaint against the threat to all of Christendom caused by "the insolence of the Jews, their crimes and their patrons at the court." The letter is full of exaggeration and polemics. It alleged that Everard's emissaries had sown disorder, trouble, and tumult everywhere they went:

They were dreadful to the Christians and kind to the Jews, . . . they have only strengthened the faction which persecutes the church. They ordered the governor of the province to protect the Jews from me. Although the safe-conduct letters were read aloud in your hallowed name and appeared to be affixed with your seal, I do not believe that they were decreed by your wisdom . . . through this the Jews triumphed greatly, and the Christians were dejected. . . . The demands of the Jews have been approved to such an extent that they dare to preach to the Christians about what they should believe and regard as true, and they curse God and the Savior in the presence of Christians. This perversity is abetted by the emissaries, who are alleged to have said that the Jews are by no means as contemptible as many believe, but that they are dear to you and preferable to the Christians. . . . Distinguished personages ask them for a prayer and a blessing, thereby acknowledging that they value the Jewish law more highly. . . . The Jews produce letters written in your name and with your seal, which we regard as forgeries; their women strut about in clothes allegedly given them by ladies in the imperial family and in the capital; they proclaim the glory of their forefathers and, contrary to the law, have received permission to build new synagogues; and it has reached the point that uninformed Christians prefer the Jewish rabbis to our own priests. . . . Since it is a fact that the Jews live among us, and since we should neither bear them ill will nor bring harm to their life, health, or property, we ought to strictly observe the regulations of the church as to when we must be on our guard against them and when we may approach them as fellow human beings. Therefore I must stress again what the Frankish church and its leaders, kings as well as bishops, have decreed concerning the separation of the two religions, specifically in the records that are in harmony with the authority and deeds of the apostles and that go back to the Old Testament. This evidence shows the abhorrence with which these enemies of truth must be viewed. . . .

Agobard advocated the strictest enforcement of the older regulations in order to separate completely the Jews from the Christians—socially, economically, and intellectually; he claimed that from the pulpit he had made every endeavor to reach this goal. He especially deplored the slave trade that extended over the entire Mediterranean. Agobard confessed that Christians were also involved as buyers and sellers, but he seemed to lay the blame exclusively on the Jews.

In order to impress the emperor with theological and legal arguments, Agobard convoked an assembly of bishops. The result was a treatise of twenty-seven chapters, which Agobard sent to the emperor. The work, regarded as the fourth letter, is a review of the relevant decrees of the Frankish church and the scriptural passages on which the decisions were based. The treatise does not go into the practical problem at all but presents only theological and legal evidence. Agobard's presentation of the legal position is complete and systematic; the reasoning is compelling and the demands are legal. The older rules were a part of canon law. The safe-conduct letters and the tolerant attitude of the imperial court had indeed limited canon law, which in these matters went as far back as the Roman emperor Justinian, who died in A.D. 565.

The justification that Agobard sought to derive from the scriptures is interesting. He could cite only two direct quotes of Jesus, the meaning of which, moreover, is disputed. He reminded the reader that Jesus at first had addressed himself only "to the lost sheep of the house of Israel" (Matthew 10:6), but after his resurrection had ordered his disciples to go into all the world and baptize all creation (Mark 16:15 ff.). The second passage is Jesus's lament over Chorazin, Bethsaida, and Capernaum (Matthew 11:21). Agobard tried to prove by these passages that Jesus himself repudiated the Jews. But he took his principal argument from the book of Acts and the letters of the apostles—documents from a period in which our problem had already reached the stage of open conflict and rivalry. It is not difficult to find historical proof in the book of Acts of the growing hostility between the Jewish synagogue and the new Christian congregations, which, to some extent, consisted of Jews. Agobard did not overlook a single one of these passages. He quoted the words of Paul (Acts 13:46 ff.): "It was necessary that the word of God should be spoken first to you [the Jews]. Since you thrust it from you, and judge yourselves unworthy of eternal life, behold, we turn to the Gentiles. For so the Lord has commanded us, saying, 'I have set you to be a light for the Gentiles, that you may bring salvation to the uttermost parts of the earth.' "

For Agobard this passage was the ultimate consequence of Jesus's teachings. Agobard made no distinction between the Christian commandment to love one's enemy and the understandable human animosity with which the apostles reciprocated the natural hostility of the Jews. On the contrary, he wanted to make the cause of the apostles against the Jews his own and felt called upon, as heir and successor to the apostles, to carry out the judgment they had pronounced. The argument had clearly moved away from religious thoughts and had intensified to the pathos of the *ecclesia triumphans*. It becomes more and more difficult to distinguish the bishop's religious sincerity from his desire for power; his righteousness from his vengeance. The Jews' rationalistic criticism of Jesus's character and resurrection was magnified in the eyes of the bishop to a persecution threatening the foundation of the Christian faith. This offensive provocation could be countered, according to the bishop, only by a complete segregation of the Jews from the Christians. This fourth letter hardly refers to the actual problem that gave rise to it; the political ambition of this prince of the church is concealed behind theological argumentation. Agobard hid the open hostility under the pretense of religious zeal.

Finally, in the fifth and final letter, Agobard addressed himself to his episcopal colleagues. In this last letter he said what he really meant and gave himself up to his antagonistic rhetoric: "It seems degrading to our faith and is even injurious to it that the sons of light are blackened by the association with darkness, and that the church, which should be spotless and flawless in preparation for the embrace of the divine beloved, sullies itself by its association with the infamous, loathsome, and depraved Synagoga. And it is preposterous that the chaste maiden, the bride of Christ, should beg that whore for bread. . . ." Agobard proposed measures to the bishops for the complete isolation of the Jews and confirmed the emperor's indifference to canon law. The absolute claims of the church on the state and society are clearly perceptible in his words. The letter, which was not intended for a wider audience, gives an idea of what the sermons that Agobard preached on the relationships between Christians and Jews may have been like.

With regard to the *Altercatio*, we have pointed out the significance of the slow transformation of Ecclesia and Synagoga: as biblical expressions and religious allegories both became living creatures endowed with human virtues and vices. This personification of a religious principle, which is especially clear in the idea of the *unio mystica* and the rejection of Synagoga, projects this principle to the level of real life: the symbols become reality; medieval Jewry is identified with the alleged failure of the Old Testament doctrine and made responsible for it. Agobard's last letter reflects closely the language and spirit of the *Altercatio*. The earlier letters set forth the problem in the theological and legal terms of the time. However, personal animosity and political ambition are revealed increasingly, until in the last letter all considerations are gone.

A sixth letter, again addressed to the emperor, is traditionally attributed to Agobard. This letter, however, was written by his like-minded successor, Amulo, who used Agobard's letters as tracts and sermons—certainly not the only one to do so. Under Lothair and Charles the Bald, the state had made sweeping concessions to the church. It was at that time that the sixth letter was written. It reflects the coming change: priests preached in the synagogues at regular intervals, and in some dioceses force was used to make "proselytes." The letter discloses the fact that Jews in Lyons had sent their children to Arles, where there was less pressure. Amulo admonished the Bishop of Arles to see to it that these children were baptized and thus "freed from the power of unbelieving and evil minds."

Nevertheless, it would be a mistake to judge Agobard's historical role only on the basis of his five letters against the Jews. These letters must be understood in the context of his personality and his time. Many of Agobard's writings—concerning the necessity for uniform legislation in the Frankish Empire, the many types of superstition, and the worthlessness of idolatry—reveal his considerable intelligence and the influence of the Carolingian Renaissance on him. His rejection of allegorical and mystical interpretations of the Bible clearly separates him from the actual Middle Ages. On the other hand, he anticipates the later claim to papal supremacy; he is one of the first to defend the validity of a clerical office even in the hands of an unworthy priest. Progressive and conservative traits are thus combined in a very personal way. As a prince of the church he did everything possible to defend the canon law of the Frankish church against the state and to restore the former church possessions that had been lost in war and in the spreading feudalism. As a pastor he felt responsible for a people still deeply rooted in heathenism and devoted to all kinds of superstitions; and he discovered that his protégés were not equal to the confrontation with the older doctrine and world-wide culture of Judaism. It is for this last reason that he demanded the complete isolation of the Jews. Finally, as a man of his time, he could not avoid taking a stand in the factional struggle. It was apparent that the weakness of the imperial regime, due to the vacillating character of Louis, was being exploited from all sides and would inevitably lead to the formation of individual positions of power. The factional struggle explains the increasing polemics and bitterness in the letters.

There is little evidence that Agobard influenced the world of his time. His position on the Jewish question is a symptom; it was emulated sporadically in some archdioceses, and we know of some compulsory baptisms. But in general, untroubled times continued for the Jews. In Germany, they spread out as far as Austria and Bohemia during the tenth and first half of the eleventh centuries, and we know of only occasional expulsions. Favorable conditions also prevailed in the Arabic states of Spain. This peaceful existence of the Jews was due primarily to the independent secular power in these parts of Europe. Especially in Germany, the church was only one of the institutions which surrounded the throne. The Saxon and Salian kings had firmly established the rights of the state over the church. Tendencies such as those in Agobard's writings are not completely lacking, but they were, as in the Carolingian era, limited to certain groups of the clergy.

Two events changed this equilibrium drastically. One was the election of the monk Hildebrand (Pope Gregory VII) to the papacy in 1073. Gregory VII became the ardent champion of clerical omnipotence; his goal was the undisputed dominance of the papacy not only over the church and its corporate bodies, but also over secular power. Jesus's charge to Peter, "Tend my sheep" (which has been received in turn by each of Peter's successors) was understood by Gregory as a granting of unlimited power to the papacy. The precious, always temporary, equilibrium of secular and ecclesiastical power, which, although much contested, had prevailed for several centuries, was now threatened by the claims of total supremacy on the part of the papacy. It claimed to be not only the keeper of the church, but also the guardian in all secular matters. This first claim to total authority in the history of Europe undermined secular power especially in Germany, whose kings since the time of Charlemagne had been "Roman emperors."

The second event affecting the equilibrium was the crusades. These were like a natural disaster because they completely changed the living conditions of the Jews and threatened them with a religious war in all of Christendom.

Chapter 7

From the Crusades to the Ghetto

At Darun you had found me with the child.
But you will hardly know that just before
In Gath the Christians slaughtered all the Jews
With wives and children; know not, that among
These Jews my wife with seven hopeful sons
Was domiciled within my brother's house,
Sent to him for safekeeping, where they all
Were burned to death.
—LESSING, *Nathan the Wise*

The crusades were not the first religious wars of the Middle Ages. The fight gainst the infidels had always been regarded as meritorious. Under the banner of the cross, military campaigns were waged against the non-Christian world. The campaigns of Charlemagne against the Arabs and the heathen Saxons and the wars with the Hungarians, Slavs, and Wends were also church undertakings. But the Jews who lived as minorities among the people of Europe were not then considered heathen; indeed, the *Concordia* placed them in proximity to and under the protection of Christianity. The Good Friday liturgy prescribed a prayer for them. The bond of beliefs that they shared with the Christians was still recognized. That bond was rent in the year 1096 when religious fanatics came forth with the idea that the war of extermination against "the enemies of Christ" had to begin at home.

The excesses of the crusaders toward the Jews were the consequence of a contradictory situation centuries old and charged with conflict. The practice of any religion is characterized externally by the service of worship. When this service is bound up inseparably with the life of the individual and the group and is manifested daily, and when public attitudes insist on conformity—as often happens in times of great movements and aspirations—a divergent religious position will in itself arouse opposition. To be sure, the church had preached tolerance toward the Jews for centuries. But at the same time, it had proceeded with great severity against heretical movements in the church itself and at times against heathens as well. In this lay an apparent contradiction. The distinctions that could explain it were too fine for the masses and could easily be denied. The people, who were now swept up in the crusades, were neither able nor willing to make these distinctions. Ignorance combined with the mass psychosis of a popular movement and its demagogues. The dangerous fallacy in the minds of the crusaders appeared to a contemporary German-Jewish chronicler as follows:[1] "Behold, we go forth to find the Holy Sepulcher and avenge ourselves on the Israelites; and here are the Jews, who killed Him and crucified Him without cause. Let us take revenge on them first and wipe them out so that they no longer are a people and the name of Israel is no longer mentioned; or they must become like us and profess our faith. . . ."

In the minds of many Christians who were ready to serve God with the sword, the complex idea of *Concordia* could scarcely assert itself. Why should an exception be made of the Jews at a time when the church had become increasingly intolerant toward those of differing religious opinions? For a large number of overzealous pilgrims, this was the opportunity to earn the honor of the crusades right at home instead of in the Orient. It was a primitive, tempting urge to take personal initiative in punishing the Jews for Christ's death by destroying the Jewish communities or forcing them to accept baptism. The slogan of the Jews' guilt in the death of Christ was from then on the driving force behind the pogroms. The original, genuine religious conflict had been pushed aside and replaced by an expression of hatred that presented itself as a slogan for military zeal and harshness.

To be sure, the leaders of the crusades, kings, and secular and ecclesiastical princes firmly opposed these outrages (for example, Henry IV in 1096 and Frederick Barbarossa in 1189), and we know from contemporary sources that part of the population stood by the Jews in their plight and offered them refuge. But the terror recurred during each crusade with dreadful regularity. Even Bernard of Clairvaux, whose religious genius had inspired European knighthood to undertake the Second Crusade, was for a time powerless against this spirit of vengeance, superstition, and fanaticism. These excesses destroyed the last vestiges of life still dormant in the *Concordia*, and ushered in a new era in the relationship of the two religions. Humiliation, suppression, and naked force in every form became the custom and were accepted in the course of time as justifiable. The desire for communality was extinct.

The following quotations are taken from contemporary German historians:

While all of creation called out for service to the Creator, the devil sowed weeds along with the good seed, awakened false prophets and mixed false brethren among God's warriors under the cloak of religions. . . . At that time Count Emicho, notorious for his tyrannical fury, appeared on the Rhine asserting that, like a second Saul, he had been inspired to his new mission through divine revelation, and arrogated to himself the leadership of nearly 12,000 crusaders. As the latter passed through the cities on the Rhine, the Main, and the Danube, they tried to prove their zeal for Christianity by also endeavoring either to destroy completely the accursed Jews wherever they came upon them or to drive them into the arms of the church.

In Mainz they slew nine hundred Jews, sparing neither women nor children. The bishop of this city at the time was Rothard, to whom the Jews had fled with their valuables for protection; however, neither the bishop nor his knights, who happened to be present in considerable number, were able to defend the Jews and rescue them from the crusaders, perhaps because Christians did not want to fight against Christians on behalf of Jews. After they stormed the bishop's castle, where the Jews had sought refuge, and even the chambers of the bishop, they murdered all the Jews they found there. This massacre took place on the Tuesday before Whitsunday; it was a sorry sight as they transported the large and numerous piles of corpses out of town on wagons. The Jews in Cologne, Worms, and other cities in Germany and France were murdered in the same way. Only a few escaped, who took refuge in baptism in their plight; and yet the Jews, more than any other people, should not be forced to believe against their will.[2]

Similar atrocities happened everywhere along the crusaders' line of march. The establishment of the Kingdom of Jerusalem was sealed with the death of the Jews living there; they were either burned to death in their synagogues or they bought their survival by surrendering their property or accepting baptism.

These events strengthened the Jews' memory of their national and religious past, the captivity, and the persecutions during their long history. These memories created a will to resist beyond the grave. The hymns sung in the synagogues at that time are moving documents of a deeply rooted spiritual resistance. A Jewish hymn of penitence and lament contains the following passage: "We are reviled and spat upon, treated like the dirt in the alleys; we sit silently in our corners like a witness in court, convicted of lying; we hear the mockery and give no answer. . . ." Both Jewish and Christian historical sources relate the voluntary deaths of entire Jewish communities, who preferred this ultimate consequence to being subjected to forced baptism. Men, women, and children fled to the synagogues. Threatened with death if they refused baptism, they slew one another: an action understood by their contemporaries as a sacrifice for their belief. A lament composed by Kalomynos ben Juda, a liturgical poet who wrote in Mainz after 1100, reads as follows:

> . . . The noble women make haste,
> That their children bleed as sacrifices,
> Fathers quickly slaughter their sons,
> And do not spare their own lives.
> To extol your oneness
> Young and beautiful women sacrifice their lives;
> "Hear, Israel!" their lips tremble
> And "The only God" is the last sound
> From the bridegroom and his bride:
> Thus, those devoted to each other in life
> Have achieved union in their sacrificial death.[3]

The appeal to the one God, to whom this sacrifice is made, appears repeatedly in these hymns. For the Jews, this was the ultimate decision which could not be evaded; and who could deny that in such a situation this decision was more natural and historically truer than the crusaders' threats of "baptism or death" and the so often misused "God wills it."

A German historical source dating from the year 1096 reports:

> In their fury the masses proceeded first to persecute the Jews in the cities and in their strongholds, or wherever else they lived; they tried to force them to believe in Jesus Christ as God, or they would lose their life at once. When these fanatical mobs advanced on Trier, the Jews living there expected a fate similar to that which their fellow believers had already suffered in other places. Some of them stabbed their own children to death, saying that they wanted to protect them from the Christian madness and that it would be better to send them back to Abraham's bosom. Some Jewish women went to the river and, filling their bodices and sleeves with stones, leaped off the bridge. The remainder, who sought to save their lives, took their belongings and their children and fled to the palace, the sanctuary in Trier where Bishop Egilbert was staying at the time, and tearfully implored his protection. The bishop called upon the Jews to become converts, and they declared themselves ready to accept baptism so that they might escape the clutches of their pursuers.[4]

The kings of France, Germany, and England did everything within their power to prevent this rash and fatal action. Henry IV upheld the rights of the German Jews. Some of the more powerful cities defended their Jews from the crusaders and made it a point of honor that no Jew was harmed within their walls without due process of law. Before Frederick Barbarossa set out for the Holy Land in 1188, he took strict measures to protect the Jews, as did Richard the Lion-Hearted, who was, however, unsuccessful in this regard. His departure for the Orient was soon followed by mass executions of the Jews in England. On the whole, the secular powers attempted to take systematic action in order to suppress these constantly recurring outbreaks. The Jews were finally placed under the direct and sole jurisdiction of the king by being declared in the royal domain, as happened in Germany from 1179 on. This measure took the place of the safe-conduct letters of the Carolingian era and extended this protection to all Jews. It was the only possible countermove. Yet it was of dubious value, for the protective obligation of the king was purchased with high taxes, and in time the Jews became the living property of the ruler.[5]

It was not uncommon for a king to pawn these assets to princes, bishops, or cities and grant them the right to financially exploit the property of the Jews. The capital value that Judaism represented became, in the hands of various patrons, a decisive factor in the political and economic developments of the late Middle Ages. The rulers' right and that of princes and dignitaries of the realm to use this capital in his own interest was not contested and was commonly exercised from the thirteenth century on. Finally, the Jew, like the serf, was limited in his freedom of movement to the boundaries of his guardian's territory. He not only lost touch with other European Jews, but he also failed to find a true home in his surroundings. He was gradually restricted to an isolated, sectarian existence that materialized later in the ghetto.

Isolation forms the character of a people—indeed, the character of both the isolated and the non-isolated. All relationships are endangered. Intolerance, ignorance, and superstition are the consequence. The charge of ritual murder was made for the first time in 1171; soon thereafter came the accusation of desecration of the sacrament. Such charges were made regularly, accompanied by references to other forms of sacrilege for which the Jews were increasingly made to suffer. The church itself seemed to sanction the spirit of violence against those of a different faith. The thirteenth century was characterized not only by occasional forced conversions of Jews, but also by the systematic campaign to exterminate the Albigenses. The same Lateran Council that established the Inquisition ordered the Jews to wear certain distinguishing apparel;[6] Pope Innocent III declared that the Jews were forever destined by God to slavery as a punishment for the death of Christ: thus, an idea that had originated in 1096 in the minds of misguided pilgrims was incorporated into the venerable system of the spiritual universe. St. Thomas Aquinas incorporated the enslavement of the Jews in his legal teachings: the church, kings, and princes had the right to dispose of the possessions of the Jews as if these possessions were their own property. The ultimate ideological step had been taken: an originally religious principle had resolved into social, political, and economic concepts and claims and had thus been deprived of its real meaning. The local authorities, princes, or cities, which by royal privilege were guardians of the Jews, gradually excluded them from the guilds and the mercantile class, from property ownership, and from association with Christians. Soon the Jews found themselves limited to an occupation that the church did not permit Christians to engage in (the church not always being consistent in this restriction)—namely, the lending of money at usurious interest. This occupation finally identified the Jews with the abuses and crises of early capitalism, of which the Jews were the beneficiaries and often the victims.

Through the social and economic mechanism that was then brought into play, Christianity retreated from the *Concordia.* The Old Testament was restricted to its theological significance, which no longer cast any light on the lives of the Jews. They ceased to be the "descendants of the patriarchs and prophets" and were regarded instead as the "murderers of Christ." They easily became victims of public excitement, expectation, or fear. Sometimes, even the establishment of a new church holiday brought affliction and persecution, as, for example, happened in the first jubilee year of 1300. Accusations of ritual sacrifice of human life, desecration of the Host, and witchcraft became more common,[7] followed by confiscation, execution, and the burning of synagogues, books, and sacred implements. The greatest atrocities broke out in the year 1349, when the devastation and horrors of the Black Death, the Indian plague, were blamed on the Jews, and the populace in all of Europe avenged itself on them. In Germany alone, more than eighty Jewish communities were extirpated, a shocking triumph of ignorance, superstition, and hatred, which was, in many places, followed by impetuous outbreaks of public contrition and penance—both symptoms of the loss of the equilibrium of religious and social justice.[8]

In the midst of this decay there were, however, courageous and thoughtful voices as well, which sought to end this disastrous trend and to uncover once more the sources of religious insight. Bernard of Clairvaux, a mystic and preacher who had considerable influence on leading political figures, brought about, in the year 1148, a temporary end to the persecution in some areas. Just as the crudade of 1096 had led to acts of violence against the Jews, the enthusiasm—which was Bernard's doing—for the crusade pledged in 1145 had evoked a similar reaction. The wave of terror had been organized in a powerful movement on the Rhine. The sermon in which Bernard checked this movement by the force of his words and even converted the ringleader is not preserved, but finds an echo in one of his letters:

We have heard and we rejoice that you are aglow with divine fervor; yet the standard of knowledge must not be lacking. The Jews must not be persecuted and slaughtered—not even driven away. Consult the sacred scripture and you will find something new prophesied in Psalm 59:10–11 about the Jews: "my God will let me look in triumph on my enemies. Slay them not, lest my people forget." They are for us like a living document recording the passion of our Master. They are thus scattered all over the world, so that they may be witnesses to our redemption while they suffer the just punishment for such a misdeed. For this reason, too, the church [Ecclesia] adds in that psalm: "make them totter by thy power, and bring them down, O Lord, our shield!" [Verse 11]. Thus it has come to pass: they have been scattered and thrust down, and suffer harsh captivity at the hands of the Christian princes. Yet in the evening they will repent, and then their reward will not be wanting. And finally, when the full number of the Gentiles have come in, all Israel will be saved, as the apostle says [Romans 11:25–26]. Whoever dies in the meanwhile will naturally remain in death.[9]

Thus Bernard rejected vengeance here on earth, relegating it to the judgment day—the eschatological expectation. He revived the teachings of the church fathers, in somewhat the way they had already been stated by Origen: "The Jews are and remain our brothers, who will not join us, to be sure, until later—namely, when we, by virtue of our teachings and exemplary lives, have moved them to emulate us."

Bernard based this eschatological expectation on the epistle of Paul to the Romans, in which a basic idea of *Concordia*, inspired by the Old Testament prophets, found its purest expression:

Lest you be wise in your own conceits, I want you to understand this mystery, brethren. A hardening has come upon part of Israel, until the full number of the Gentiles come in, and so all Israel will be saved; as it is written, "The Deliverer will come from Zion, he will banish ungodliness from Jacob"; "and this will be my covenant with them when I take away their sins." As regards the gospel they are enemies of God, for your sake; but as regards election they are beloved for the sake of their forefathers [Romans 11:25–28].

God still loves the people of Israel and will not take back his promise.

This basic idea, revived by Bernard in a critical hour, remained alive in sermons and in pastoral work; it would not be possible otherwise to explain the literary and artistic development of our theme. Almost one hundred years later, the eschatological idea can still be found in sermons, though colored by the views of the time. Thus Berthold of Regensburg, the great preacher who lived about the middle of the thirteenth century, expressed the hatred for the Jews current at that time. He was driven by his ardent opposition to usury and by his concern for the "flock" entrusted to his care. "He is fearful because the Jews keep their faith better than the Christians." [10] But the following passage is also found in his writings:

They [the princes] must protect the lives and property of the Jews as well as the Christians, for they are included in the peace. Whoever slays a Jew must atone to both God and his worldly judge, as if he had murdered a Christian, because the emperors have taken them into the peace.[11] We tolerate the Jews among Christians for two reasons. One is that they are witnesses to the fact that our Lord was martyred by them. When a Christian sees a Jew he should ponder this devoutly. "Ah," he should think, "are you one of those at whose hands our Lord Jesus Christ was martyred and suffered for our sins?" And you should thank God for His suffering, you Christian people, when you see the Jew. You must never forget His suffering, for He never forgets us. Yet we should be especially reminded of this by the Jews. And there is another reason: all of them who survive after the death of the antichrist will become Christians before judgment day. . . .

The relationship of Christian to Jew had become purely a matter of conscience. The thought is clearly expressed that Christ's death on the cross is continually being caused by the eternally sinful nature of man—including all of Christendom.

In a fifteenth-century hymn this train of thought is carried through to its conclusion:

> It is our great sin and grievous misdeeds
> that nailed Jesus the true Son of God to the cross.
> For this reason we must not revile you,
> Poor Judah, and the host of Jews. The guilt is indeed ours.[12]

Here we can end our survey of the relationship between Christians and Jews in the Middle Ages. The theme of Ecclesia and Synagoga had ceased to be religious; it had disappeared in the tumult of social struggles and was discernible only with difficulty. The "Jewish question" took the place of the religious problem. It was seldom viewed in anything but the political and economic sense; the deeper layers remained buried. Even in later times, among thoughtful intellects disposed to soul-searching and forbearance, this deeper layer was no longer reached. The guilt feelings of the Christian seemed to be limited to the economic, or, at best, the moral aspect of the problem, as stated in a document that appeared in 1590:

> How could the Jews have brought about so much mischief and destruction with their usury, money dealing, and all their other financial manipulations, if Christians everywhere had not aided them; had not needed them because of their idleness, ostentation, and extravagance; and indeed had not sought them out and taken part in their usurious enterprises? People accuse the Jews alone and do not say as they rightly should: *Mea maxima culpa*, my own guilt is greatest.[13]

Chapter 8

The Drama of the Antichrist and the Prophet Play

Strictly speaking, there is nothing theatrical
that is not, at the same time, visually symbolic:
a meaningful action that suggests
an even more meaningful one.
—GOETHE

I

The historical documents and movements with which we are concerned were still isolated and often unrelated in the early Middle Ages. Yet they all derive from the same roots and testify to both the theoretical and actual attitudes of Christian society toward the Jewish minority. The symptomatic importance of these fragments cannot be denied.

In the eleventh century the theme of Ecclesia and Synagoga acquired sharper features. The interaction between various areas of life became visible to the extent that the medieval civilization emerged as a unique social and intellectual system. Problems of scholastic theology—for example, the controversy over the sacraments—had a direct effect on religious observance, and the concept of papal supremacy had immediate social and political consequences. This intellectual ferment was portrayed in art, the "mirror of the world," which reflected the essential experiences of medieval man. Within this growing system of ideas and doctrines, of symbols and forms, Ecclesia and Synagoga assumed a prominent position and developed their innate dispositions to the point of dramatic and artistic greatness. This was at the very time the Middle Ages reached its climax in the crusades.

The liturgy for church holidays and the respective biblical passages contained many dramatic elements, especially for Easter and Christmas. The sequence in the Easter mass had developed antiphonal chanting in which the conversation between the three women and the angel at the holy sepulchre was presented. This scene of the three women at the sepulchre, acted out by clerics, was fully developed as early as 970;[1] it was the germ cell of the medieval Easter play and of the later passion play. Even as late as the eighteenth century, Goethe made use of the scene: from the nearby church the choirs of angels, women, and disciples can be heard proclaiming to Faust the "first solemn hour of the Easter festival." The "lament of Mary" is another dramatic Easter motif; it too was incorporated into the passion play. The ceremonial representation humanized the mystery of the Easter message through words, gestures, and music and gradually developed an independent existence and artistic form of its own. The Easter liturgy proved quite fruitful: Pontius Pilate, Lucifer, Peter, and other characters enlarged the presentation with new scenes. With the figure of Christ the actual passion play became complete; this, however, did not occur until a relatively late date.

The same development took place in the case of the Christmas play, but even greater freedom in regard to the liturgical text. The meeting of the three wise men with Herod, their adoration of the child, their dream and return home, and the slaying of the children in Bethlehem are the oldest scenes in the Christmas play; like the Easter scenes, they can also–individually or in sequence–be traced back to the tenth century.

Within this context the *Sermo*, whose messianic prophecies are part of the celebration of Christ's birth, began to be dramatized. From the *Sermo*, the *Ordo Prophetarum* (the prophet play) evolved as a prelude to the birth of Christ. To be sure, the bitter polemics of the *Sermo* were also introduced into the Christmas play. The Jews are summoned before the "Reader" while the prophets appear in person one after another, take positions around the Reader, and repeat their prophecies and visions. In later versions, the number of witnesses increased. In some, the Jews are led by their elder, the Archisynagogus, as spokesman, while the Reader—often St. Augustine himself—becomes the leader and spokesman for the prophets. The conflict thus became centered on just two figures, and the moment was inevitable when Ecclesia and Synagoga would themselves assume these roles in the prophet play. But this did not occur until relatively late, at a time that cannot be exactly determined. For it was not the prophet play that first brought Ecclesia and Synagoga together in person on the stage, but rather the *Ludus de Antichristo*, the drama of the antichrist, written about the middle of the twelfth century for the imperial court of Frederick Barbarossa and presented there. This drama, when contrasted with the prophet play, testifies to the high state of the dramatic art and its growing thematic variety.

II

Even the most elementary dramatic undertaking requires a certain measure of internal unity and consistency in the characterization: delivery, expressions, and gestures should be fused into a distinctive whole. Drama has a different artistic dimension from that of sermon and scripture. The unknown authors of the religious drama found the texts already prescribed in biblical passages, in hymns, and in religious legends. From the words of the text, acting and suffering man himself was supposed to emerge. In the drama, however, words and actions, grief and joy, delusion and devotion vied with each other to please the eye and the ear and to satisfy both religious imagination and ordinary curiosity. Yet, at the same time, the play had to remain within the tradition and to preserve the venerable wording of the text.

In the beginning, the religious drama was exclusively the work of the clergy: the words were in Latin and the performance was part of the worship service. But in examining the sacred stories with regard to their dramatic potential and in presenting them year after year, new objects of popular veneration were discovered and given dramatic form. New possibilities for worshipping and experiencing God were revealed in the ancient texts; intellectual and spiritual values became visible. This increased as soon as laymen replaced the clergy in the roles in church drama and presented the plays in the vernacular. The discovery of the dramatic possibilities in the natural expressiveness of the human face and the great masterpieces of physiognomic sculpture in the thirteenth century derive from a common source. The early religious drama did not fail to have its influence on the spiritual expressiveness and physiognomic interest in sculpture and literature. Closely related to this experience and visualization of human existence are the vivid characterizations in Wolfram's *Parzival*, Gottfried's *Tristan*, and Hartmann von Aue's *Poor Henry*, as well as in the monumental statuary in Strasbourg, Bamberg, or Naumburg.

The extent and effect of the drama is also demonstrated by the opposition it evoked. Gerhoh von Reichersberg, a learned cleric in the twelfth century, strongly criticized the presentation of drama in the churches. We learn from his polemics[2] that "men of ecclesiastical rank and high education" portrayed "the birth of Jesus, the Virgin Mary in childbirth, the slaughter of the innocent children, the lament of Rachel, and the appearance of the antichrist." Clerics also played the roles of devils, women, and soldiers. Gerhoh saw great danger in this, asserting that no one could convincingly play the part of a devil, let alone the antichrist, without also being inwardly drawn to the nature and reality of such a role. Gerhoh thus revealed an insight into the nature of the dramatic art that links him to Plato and Pascal. His objection was based on personal experience: he himself had taken part in religious dramas in his youth and had, no doubt, felt in himself the transforming power of dramatic and poetic illusion.

Gerhoh's testimony is extremely valuable, for it documents the suggestive power of medieval drama. The reason he disapproved of it was the same reason it finally prevailed: the physical representation of the sacred events was, for the viewers, proof of their reality. The play was a spiritual force superior to the material world and able to transform it, ennoble it, or even to ward it off. The Oberammergau passion plays, which originated as late as 1634 in a vow made in the face of an impending plague, were a last attempt to ward off the harsh realities of earthly life through the magic of physical representations.

Although the beginnings of medieval drama may appear to us as quite narrow and limited in motif, they nevertheless drew their strength from the same source as did the classical drama of world literature—the transforming power of poetic illusion. Thus, despite the controversy, there was a consensus between Gerhoh and Plato, St. Augustine, and Pascal: the desire to free supernatural reality—the divine concept—from worldly limitations—its human interpretation. This relationship of idea and image, their harmony and contradiction, must be kept in mind if we are to comprehend the appearance of Ecclesia and Synagoga on the stage—first in the drama of the antichrist and later in the prophet plays.

III

The medieval mind was constantly preoccupied with thoughts concerning the end of the world. The concept of the foe who would appear prior to the end derived from the prophetic tradition of the Jews and reached a high point in the New Testament where the imposing synopsis of atrocities, oppression, and judgment are reported in each of the first three Gospels. Wars and conquest, earthquakes and plagues, persecution of the faithful, and temptation by false prophets are the signs of the coming judgment: "And then if any one says to you, 'Look, here is the Christ!' or 'Look, there he is!' do not believe it. False Christs and false prophets will arise and show signs and wonders, to lead astray, if possible, the elect. But take heed; I have told you all things beforehand" (Mark 13:21–23). "And this gospel of the kingdom will be preached throughout the whole world, as a testimony to all nations; and then the end will come" (Matthew 24:14). "And then they will see the Son of man coming in clouds with great power and glory. . . . Heaven and earth will pass away, but my words will not pass away" (Mark 13:26 and 31). The book of Revelation and the letters of Paul also proclaim the great eschatological expectation:

Let no one deceive you in any way; for that day will not come, unless the rebellion comes first, and the man of lawlessness is revealed, the son of perdition, who opposes and exalts himself against every so-called god or object of worship, so that he takes his seat in the temple of God, proclaiming himself to be God. . . . And then the lawless one will be revealed, and the Lord Jesus will slay him with the breath of his mouth and destroy him by his appearing and his coming [II Thessalonians 3:4 and 8].

Among the peoples of the Germanic North the biblical eschatology combined with pagan views. The terrifying figure of the antichrist came into being, who, in a final advance of godlessness, gains mastery of the earth for a short time. This theme emerges as early as the ninth century in the Old High German verses of the "Muspilli," in which the antichrist is finally conquered by Elijah. But the latter is also mortally wounded, and his blood drips down to earth from the heavenly battlefield, setting the earth on fire. The verses of the "Muspilli" well up in a grandiose vision of the end of the world and the last judgment:

When Elijah's blood drips down to earth
The mountains catch fire and not a tree remains standing
On the earth; the waters dry up,
The moor is swallowed, heaven smoulders in the flame;
The moon falls, and man's homestead burns.
No stone remains standing; the tribunal of judgment
Goes forth with fire to punish the flesh.
No man can save another from the Muspilli.
When far and wide everything is consumed by the rain of fire
And swept away by fire and wind
Where, then, is the boundary that one has once contested with his relatives?
It is consumed by fire, as the soul is by grief;
The latter knows not how to do penance and thus goes to perdition.

One may be reminded of the vision of the end of the world in the "Völuspa," the opening poem of the Old Icelandic *Elder Edda*, though this work was not put into written form until the thirteenth century. These visions loomed over the centuries of medieval life like a menacing admonition. From time to time it was proclaimed, and believed, that the last judgment was imminent, and whole generations were converted and did penance—as happened, for example, about the turn of the first Christian millennium. Again, in the Reformation era, the young Dürer in the Germanic North carved his woodcuts of the apocalypse and drew his "Battle of the Archangel Michael with the Dragon," a work that seems like an illustration of the vision that appeared more than 600 years before in the "Muspilli." At the same time Luca Signorelli was painting "The Days of the Antichrist" in the cathedral of Orvieto.

In the tenth century, the expectation of the last judgment and the legend of the antichrist combined with the doctrine of the worldly empires: the last empire on earth, it was prophesied, was the medieval empire; and the last emperor would again restore it to its old splendor and glory before laying down his crown at Jerusalem in order that God alone might rule. The antichrist would take advantage of this pious renunciation of worldly power in order to establish his dominion. Through acts of violence, false wonders, and gold he would extend his power, make fire come down from heaven, cause the sea to become restless and calm it down again, and raise the dead, so that even the pious would regard him as the returning Christ. All who believed in him would be rewarded and receive a sign, the letter *A*, on their foreheads; those who resisted would be killed. The Jews would discover in him the long-awaited Messiah. Elijah and Enoch, who would oppose him, he would have killed. His rule would last three and one-half years, then God would kill him by the breath of His mouth and Christ would come to judge mankind. The reign of the antichrist was to be the last ordeal of mankind and prelude to the last judgment.

An anonymous twelfth-century German poet put this colossal theme on the stage. The *Ludus de Antichristo*[3] is a unique sort of production somewhat resembling an opera or oratorio. Words and action alternate with silent, highly dramatic scenes. It was composed in Latin and intended for the knightly aristocracy and clerical dignitaries at the royal court of the Hohenstaufen. An entirely different spirit from that of the church drama prevails in the *Ludus*: knighthood and the crusades, the struggle between emperor and pope, and the

Hohenstaufen dreams of world domination provide the magnificent and stirring historical background. A great epoch is reflected in a great genius: the author elevated the work to poetic heights unequalled in any other drama of the Middle Ages. He incorporated his own world into the portrayal of the eschatological events, describing his own time as that of the antichrist. In his drama, Frederick Barbarossa is the emperor who will reestablish the empire and then dedicate it to God. The whole world with the thrones of kings and of the pope is portrayed; in the middle of the scene stands the temple in Jerusalem with its altar. The poet and author of this theater that encompasses the world was also—two or three generations before the great statues in Bamberg and Strasbourg—the first to bring Ecclesia and Synagoga to the stage.[4] He removed the two allegorical figures from the context of the crucifixion and the *unio mystica* in order to use them for his own interpretation of the era.

IV

The breadth of spirit in the *Ludus* is revealed at the very outset in the prologue. Gentilitas (heathendom), Synagoga (Judaism), and Ecclesia (Christianity) make their solemn entry onto the stage, followed by rulers and their subjects. Before the entire assembled world, so to speak, a disputation commences among the three allegorical female figures over the validity of their religions.

Gentilitas is the first to state her doctrine: belief in one god is contrary to ancient, but still valid, human experience. The blessing of peace and the curse of war cannot possibly come from the same omnipotent will.

> "Whoever says therefore that one god
> Rules over such manifold interests,
> Must needs believe that he
> Shows his favors to hostile peoples . . .
> For this reason we perceive
> That there are different gods
> Whose duties, we observe,
> Also differ in their turn." [5]

Human reason must therefore assume the existence of different gods with various dominions; any other conclusion would end in contradiction. Gentilitas refers to historical experience and human reason; she knows nothing of revelation and mercy.

In solemn words Synagoga[6] takes exception to the Christians' false hopes for redemption. How could Jesus, who promised life, fall victim to death himself?

> " 'Tis strange if he yields to death
> Who gives life to others.
> Can any one be saved by him
> Who is not able to save himself?"

The death on the cross rules out the possibility that God became man in Jesus. Christ was, therefore, merely one of the many pagan gods.

Ecclesia, dressed as a woman and wearing a breastplate and crown, proclaims her good news antiphonally with those who follow her: Christ had superseded and overcome the law of death. She warns doubters of eternal damnation:

> "This is the faith whence life springs,
> By which the sting of death is soothed.
> If there's any one who believes differently,
> Him we condemn eternally!"

Those accompanying Ecclesia—the allegorical figures Misericordia and Justitia, the emperor and his knights, the pope and the clerics—join in proclaiming the tidings.

Only then does the play itself begin, consisting of antiphonal chanting, processions, pantomime, and group movements. The German king, who is also the Roman emperor, reestablishes the empire and ascends the highest throne. The Christian rulers, the kings of France, Greece, and Jerusalem, subject themselves to his rule and receive their lands from him as fiefs. Ecclesia puts herself under his protection. Already the crucial moment is at hand: the Sultan of Babylon establishes himself as the defender of the ancient gods and leads his armies against Jerusalem, where the Christian sect originated, in order to destroy it and restore Gentilitas to divine status.

"But we must wipe the name Christian from off the earth;
Which event we should inaugurate at once,
Here where the sect first began to spread."

Messengers of the hard-pressed King of Jerusalem hasten to the emperor, the protector of the church, who promises his help. Meanwhile, the people of Jerusalem receive solace and encouragement from heaven; an angel promises them deliverance from the heathens: "O Judah and Jerusalem, fear not, and be not dismayed" (II Chronicles 20:17).

The emperor comes to the aid of the holy city and defeats the sultan. After the victory he prays in the temple and, true to the words of the prophecy, lays down his crown and scepter before the altar:

"Receive my offering; for with a grateful heart
I entrust my imperial power to you, the King of Kings,
Through whom kings rule, and who alone
Deserve to be called Emperor, for you are the
Governor of all!"

Then the emperor returns to his kingdom and throne; Ecclesia, who had accompanied him to Jerusalem, remains there in the temple.

Thus, this first part of the *Ludus* portrays on the stage, in symbolic actions and through numerous allegories, the feudal empire of medieval times, the protective sovereignty of the emperor over the church, and the victory of the crusades. But behind these historical events, the rival religious ideas are seriously presented as they were generally experienced: the empiricism and logic of the pagan tradition that was the source of so much heresy; the Jewish opposition to the "death of God" on the cross and to the derogation of monotheism by the divinity of Jesus; finally, the Christian faith that overcomes death. Ecclesia, who, in the firm conviction of every hearer, is right, does not substantiate her viewpoint in such detail as do her opponents. However, the doomsday judgment against heretics is quoted repeatedly by the *Ecclesia triumphans:*

"If there's any one who believes differently,
Him we condemn eternally!"

As the three female figures—Gentilitas, Synagoga, and Ecclesia—repeat their introductory lines, moving about in solemn procession with their retinues, the main part of the *Ludus* begins. The "host of hypocrites" appear to prepare the way for the antichrist. They bow humbly in all directions in order to gain the people's favor. The King of Jerusalem welcomes them and listens to their counsel. Now the antichrist himself appears, accompanied by the hypocrites (Ypocrisi) [7] and the heretics (Heresi). He is not the devil, as one might expect according to the older tradition; the devil does not appear at all in the *Ludus*. The antichrist conceals ambition and lust for power under his simple leather jerkin. He leaves it to "hypocrisy" and "heresy" to prepare his rise to power. "Hypocrisy" will win over the laymen for him, while "heresy" will delude the clergy into recanting, so that finally all mankind will acknowledge him, the antichrist, as the returning savior.

> "I will therefore ascend [the throne] and subjugate kingdoms:
> The old laws I will repeal and proclaim new ones!"

The "hypocrites," who have been received hospitably by the King of Jerusalem, then draw their swords, drive their host from his throne, and crown the antichrist, hailing him in the words of the psalm: "strong is thy hand, high thy right hand" (Psalms 89:13). The throne of the antichrist is set up in the temple of the Lord; Ecclesia retreats in the face of the invaders' attacks and insults, finding refuge at the throne of the pope.

The conquest of the world continues. After Jerusalem and the temple have come under the control of the antichrist, the King of Greece gives in to the threats. The King of France is won over by gifts. "Heresy" had prepared well for this success. Both kings receive their lands as fiefs from the antichrist, and the letter *A*—the sign of the new master—is placed on their foreheads. But the power of the German king remains unshakable. The antichrist acknowledges his respect for the bravery of the Germans; threats will be of no avail; perhaps he can accomplish something with gifts:

> "Excellent in arms is the power of the Teutons,
> As their well tried valor testifies;

> Your task is to appease their king with gifts,
> For it is indiscreet to force the Teutons into war.
> They are certain destruction to all who war with them;
> Subdue them to us then with gifts if you can."

But the German king banishes the antichrist's messengers as liars and heretics, and a battle results nevertheless. The armies of the antichrist are conquered by the Germans. The brave victor, however, falls victim to the magic and false miracles: the alleged christ heals a cripple and a leper and brings back to life a man slain in battle (who, according to the stage directions, naturally only feigns death). The German king then also yields to this supernatural power, pays homage to the antichrist, and receives the letter *A* on his forehead. On behalf of the antichrist, the German king now completes the subjugation of the world. The Sultan of Babylon, who had remained true to the principles of Gentilitas and resisted the antichrist, surrenders as well.

After the domain of the antichrist has been extended over all the world by force, bribery, and false miracles, the play hastens toward its climax. Synagoga herself, accompanied by her host of Jews, steps up to the new ruler and is greeted by the "hypocrites." Her thoughts, which have been occupied for centuries with the messianic expectation, are cleverly manipulated by the antichrist's messengers. She therefore greets the antichrist as the long-awaited Messiah of Old Testament prophecy. She, too, receives the sign on her forehead, and the Promised Land is again promised her. The antichrist says:

> "With my assistance come out of thy confusion;
> I will restore to thee the land of promise.
> Behold the nations shall walk in thy light,
> And kings shall reign in peace under thy sway."

The ancient longing of Judaism seems to be fulfilled: the Messiah, who is the savior of the Christians as well, has come; heathens, Jews, and Christians have been brought together under his rule.

Because the antichrist's victory is so complete, the only one who can still resist him and restore the truth is Elijah. Long ago in ancient Israel, it was Elijah who had demolished the idols, annihilated the false prophets, and reestablished the worship of the one true God. According to ancient Jewish tradition, his return is the prognostic of the messianic era; no one is more qualified than he to unmask the antichrist. In the Old High German "Muspilli" as well, he is the one who overcomes the archenemy. Thus he also appears here, accompanied by Enoch, to proclaim salvation through Christ, who suffered under Pontius Pilate, rose from the dead, and reigns in eternity. Pointing to the antichrist, Elijah says:

> "Behold, now, the man of perdition has come
> Who has erected again the walls of Babylon the great,
> And he is not the Christ. As the Scriptures state,
> One has to see in him the chief of hypocrites."

Elijah and Enoch remove Synagoga's veil, which until then has covered her eyes; her blindness is cured and she perceives her error. Boldly she flings into the teeth of her enemy his true name, Antichrist, which no one before has dared to utter, and thereby reveals the dreadful meaning of the mysterious letter *A* on the foreheads of his followers.

> "We have verily been seduced by Antichrist
> Who falsely says that he is the Christ of the Jews!"

Overwhelmed by Elijah's testimony in this hour of decision, Synagoga finally declares her belief in Christ and his gospel. Even threats of death do not deter her:

> "We repent our sins;
> We return to the faith;
> We will suffer whatever
> Our Persecutor ordains!"

The archenemy cannot let this challenge remain unpunished; Synagoga, together with Elijah and Enoch, dies a martyr for Jesus Christ. Then, as the antichrist is boasting loudly of having conquered all his enemies, a thunderbolt smites him and he falls dead. His followers flee, and mankind assembles under the leadership of Ecclesia in the true belief, singing God's praise.

V

The antichrist drama is in many respects a remarkable document. Its significance for the medieval concept of empire and the dreams of world dominion in the Hohenstaufen era has been often noted, as has the portrayal of hypocrisy and heresy as destructive forces in society and in the church. Here we are interested in the role of Synagoga. It is she who breaks the spell of the antichrist in calling him by his true name.

The idea that the Jews were "blind" and that their minds were closed to the *re-velatio* is suggested in the language of the Gospels. It is uncertain when this expression of her blindness was made visible in the symbol of the blindfold; it is not found in older portrayals. It is a likely assumption that the author of the antichrist drama was the first to make this linguistic symbol also a visible one—without doubt, Synagoga wears a blindfold in the *Ludus* from the very outset. It is also possible that this motif entered the plastic and graphic arts by way of the stage.

From the second half of the twelfth century on, we find the blindfold as the emblem of Synagoga, just as the chalice, crown, and banner are the emblems of Ecclesia. A blindfold is a dramatic symbol: it must be untied, it must fall, in order to fulfill its meaning. A blindfold cannot represent eternal but only temporary blindness, which will come to an end when the word of God is revived and received at the decisive hour. The blindfold, which is to be untied, is a symbol of the eschatological expectation; it is one in the group of motifs surrounding the last judgment and makes clear the nature of this judgment: divine mercy.

The author of the antichrist drama followed this motif through all the levels of its meaning, arriving at an internal conclusion: Elijah will untie the blindfold and receive Synagoga again in the community of divine grace. The author assigned to Synagoga a martyr's death for the sake of Christ at the end of the world, brought to an end the schism that had developed in the belief in one God, restored respect for the venerable *Concordia Veteris et Novi Testamenti*, fulfilled the Pauline expectation of the final conversion of the Jews

(Romans 11:25–26), and portrayed visibly the words of St. Augustine: "God's righteousness, through which the believer is led to salvation, is concealed in the Old Testament, but revealed in the New Testament" (Harnack 441–*De spiritu et littera* 18). "Concealed" and "revealed": in this alternation between symbol and reality, the assertion was expressed that even under the blindfold of Synagoga the divine is concealed and will reveal and prove itself when the call is sounded.

The author of the *Ludus* elevated the significance of Synagoga above the primitive concepts of a time that gave rise to pogroms and forced conversions of Jews in all of Europe during the crusades; a time when the Jews were considered solely responsible for Christ's death. Perhaps the author was familiar with the mystical teachings of Bernard of Clairvaux,[8] who brought an end to the pogroms on the Rhine a few years earlier (see Chapter 7). The author demonstrated the unity in the biblical tradition and brought it to a culmination in the vision of the last judgment, when the grace of God unties the blindfold. He found the roots of guilt elsewhere: in hypocrisy and heresy, the destructive forces at work in the state and church.

Compared to the portrayals discussed in Chapter 1, showing Ecclesia and Synagoga at the foot of the cross, the blindfold in the *Ludus* is just as new an element as the moral and religious elevation of Synagoga. Certainly the *Concordia* influenced some of these portrayals and lent dignity and majesty even to the repudiated Synagoga. But a large number of portrayals dating from the beginning of the crusades and thereafter, show Synagoga as cruelly cast out into eternal darkness. The blindfold cannot be untied in these works that stand in sharp contrast to the tradition of *Concordia* and the antichrist drama.

VI

The development of the pseudo-Augustinian *Sermo contra Judeos* into the prophet play has been previously discussed. The prophet play was at first theological and didactic, but soon became filled with the polemics of religious conflicts. In essence the prophet play is a *disputatio*; however, the ending is predetermined: the opposition of the host of Jews is silenced and some of the Jews accept baptism.

The *disputatio's* predetermined conclusion obscured the genuine religious controversy over the basic problem of the nature of God and man.[9] The Jewish and Christian concepts of God were to confront each other, and at the focus would be the question, was Jesus God or man? Even in the later versions translated into the vernacular, we can still detect how deeply moved the prophets were by the wonder and mystery of Jesus's birth and the concept of God as the father of all men. We also sense the brooding logic of the Jews and their severe, scholarly line of reasoning in the face of experiences that defy rational analysis. The prophet play as such could have produced a clear confrontation between religious experience and scholarly ideology, but this contrast was overshadowed by the historical and social conflicts between Christians and the Jewish minorities. The adulteration of the genuine polarity by the contemporary conflict was also the reason why neither of the opposing sides in the prophet play is able to achieve a clear moral position.

The oldest vernacular text of a prophet play is found in the twelfth-century Norman play, *Adam.* In Germany no drama in the vernacular prior to the thirteenth century has been preserved. Noteworthy among the German dramas is the *Christmas Play of Benediktbeuren*, dating from about 1225, but even this is in Latin. The prophet play forms the first scene in this drama. The Jews are led by the high priest, the *arch-synagogus*, and stand facing the prophets under the leadership of St. Augustine. The subject of the controversy is Jesus's virgin birth, the possibility of which is strongly disputed by the *arch-synagogus* who makes use of derisive words, forced humor, grimaces, and crude jokes. According to the stage directions in the text, the Jews employ primarily derision and witticisms, whereas Augustine replies "in a cautious and polite tone. . . ."

The high priest and his Jews are to shout loudly when they hear the prophecies. The high priest shall then imitate the behavior of a Jew by the manner in which he holds his cane, nudges his companions, moves his head and entire body, and stamps his foot on the ground, while angrily saying to his companions:

"Tell me what the hypocrite says
This whitewashed wall
Tell me what the scoundrel declares
Who is a stranger to truth. . . .
As I hear, those people
Come to this conclusion:
A son must be born by
A maiden without a man.
Such great foolishness makes
Those people void of wisdom;
They proclaim that the camel
Is descended from the ox. . . ."

Later, the high priest says to St. Augustine:

"The fact that this virgin
Gives birth to a child without a man
Is a dishonor to nature
So that it becomes irrational." [10]

The controversy remains undecided. The Jews insist on *res neganda*, the prophets on *res miranda*. Then Augustine proclaims the birth of Christ, and the actual Christmas play begins.

There is no literary evidence that Ecclesia and Synagoga, who appeared on the stage in the twelfth-century *Ludus*, also appeared in the prophet play. The *disputatio* of the prophet play remains limited to the *arch-synagogus* and the Jews on the one hand, and Augustine and the prophets on the other, as shown in the Benediktbeuren play. The problem is reduced to the question of when and how Ecclesia and Synagoga took sides in the controversy between the prophets and the Jews. Only from the end of the thirteenth century on are literary sources available.

Art history as well can offer only speculation. As early as Carolingian times Ecclesia was portrayed with the symbols of the four evangelists; later, she appeared with the signs of the prophets—for example, on the portable altar of Gladbach Abbey (ca. 1150) and in the often restored Jesse window in

Metz. An arrangement similar to that in the prophet play seemed to be forming, but the opposite group remained composed entirely of Jews. In a miniature in the Codex Latinus 11560 (Paris, ca. 1250), the Jews and two church fathers dispute as in the prophet play, while Ecclesia presides—but Synagoga is missing (see Chapter 11). This omission is astonishing, since the two large statues of Ecclesia and Synagoga in Bamberg and Strasbourg (originating a generation after the Benediktbeuren drama) were developed not from the concept of the eschatological expectation in the *Ludus*, but from the *disputatio*.

The thematic fusion of the prophet play with the disputation between the queens was heralded as early as the Benediktbeuren drama. The disputation among heathendom, Judaism, and Christianity taken from the *Ludus* was appended as a conclusion, although this did not produce internal unity.[11]

It is a reasonable assumption that the allegorical figures of Ecclesia and Synagoga also appeared, with their emblems, as silent players in such dramas and that their presence, therefore, cannot be established from the texts. Liturgical celebrations of the church year, as well as medieval drama, contained processions and pageants in which the characters of the ecclesiastical plays took part. This fusion of the two elements was an essential precondition for the concept of the two women in the monumental statuary of the thirteenth century.[12]

The first literary trace of this fusion cannot be found until the end of the thirteenth century; that is, about a generation after the masterpieces of Bamberg and Strasbourg. From an extant fragment of a drama (partly in German and partly in Latin) concerning the assumption of the Virgin Mary, it is evident that the motif of controversy between the two women was woven into the plot.[13]

The full literary development of this controversy did not take place until the late fourteenth century: the Frankfurt Stage Directions should be noted here.[14] Even the Ahlsfeld drama and the Donau-Eschingen passion play are products of the fifteenth century.

Chapter 9

Synagoga's Blindfold

Everything that happens is a symbol,
And in portraying itself perfectly
It indicates the rest.
—GOETHE

I

The crusades widened the horizon of medieval Europe. Cultural contact with formerly Christian lands that had been lost to Islam for centuries was reestablished; and beyond these lands, new cultures were revealed that had been almost unknown until then. This broadening of the horizon presented European knighthood with new experiences and goals and opened up new possibilities in literature and art. In this connection some concepts had already been introduced that were not without significance for the birth of the Renaissance and the ideas of Humanism centuries later.

The theme of Ecclesia and Synagoga was considerably expanded due to the crusades. Through them, a religious idea that had existed only as an allegory for more than a thousand years was being confronted with contemporary events and, therefore, subjected not only to adulteration but also to reevaluation.[1] The principles inherent in the concept achieved a clarity that appeared as the culmination of the earlier development. In the church drama of the twelfth century, this occurred through the prophet play, which brings the conflict to a theologically predetermined end, as well as through the eschatological world of the *Ludus*, where the final judgment is left to God. The tragic and rash actions of the pilgrims on their way to Jerusalem, who thought they were doing their Christian duty by murdering Jews, were countered, if only occasionally, by a new tolerance arising from deeper levels of religious awareness. This was, for instance, the position of Walther von der Vogelweide. Like every medieval Christian he recognized only one true religion. But he was not restrained by dogmatic bounds and placed the decision of conscience above a casuistic moral doctrine. Before God all creatures are equal: Jew, Christian, and Mohammedan all obey him:

> Whoever without qualm would give
> lip-service to Thy ten commandments, Lord,
> and break them, violates love's true spirit.
> Many a man calls Thee his father:
> But he who would not have me for a brother
> speaks strong words arising from a feeble mind . . .
> Christians, Jews, and heathens serve Him
> who sustains all of life's wonders.[2]

This spiritual deepening is revealed most clearly in the plastic and graphic arts. Ecclesia and Synagoga were soon among the principal motifs: they appear on ivory tablets, in stained-glass windows, on church implements, in manuscript miniatures, and in monumental statuary. Whereas smaller works of art often retained the tradition of mutal hostility, the older tradition of *Concordia* reached full flower and artistic greatness in statuary.

Architecture was where the depiction of the entire story of salvation had begun. The creation and fall of man, redemption and judgment, past and future of the human race, are portrayed on portals, choir screens, and stained-glass windows. The prophets, apostles, saints, the scenes at the foot of the cross, the resurrection of the dead, the last judgment, and damnation—these were the themes of the portal statuary in which the saints of the church stand on the shoulders of the Old Testament prophets, thus giving visual expression to the venerable *Concordia Veteris et Novi Testamenti*. Ecclesia and Synagoga stand in the midst of these figures: "Medieval art . . . in the most exalted works it was able to produce, placed these two figures on the portals of its cathedrals—true embodiments of the entire doctrine of salvation." [3]

II

The previously discussed hostility [4] toward the Jewish minority is sometimes demonstrated by equating the Jews and Synagoga with the "murderers of Christ."

The Essen missal,[5] which appeared about 1100 and is now in the Landesbibliothek in Düsseldorf, is probably one of the earliest records of this attitude. Instead of a crown, Synagoga wears the pointed hat of medieval Jewry. From that time on she was to be a member of the Jewish community.[6] The instruments of Christ's death were placed in her hands: spear, sponge, jug of vinegar, and crown of thorns. She was thus portrayed by Godefroid de Claire about 1150 on the portable altar of Stavelot (now in Brussels) and in the crucifixion scene in the evangelistary from Bruchsal (now in the library at Karlsruhe, Codex I, folio 31). Through these additions Synagoga was accused of complicity in the death of Christ. In some portrayals she holds in her hands the tablets of the Ten Commandments, thus tempering the severity of the accusation: for example, in the portable altar of the Gladbach Abbey in Mönchen-Gladbach, dating from about 1150. In a window of the cathedral at Châlons-sur-Marne,[7] Synagoga appears in a half medallion beneath the crucifixion scene, blindfolded and with the instruments of torture in her hands. A banderole cites the malediction: "*Sanguis eius super nos et super filios nostros*" (His blood come over us and over our children).

The ultimate stage appears to have been reached in a picture, formerly in Copenhagen, in which the spear in Synagoga's hand breaks as she attempts to pierce the feet of Christ.[8] Even this gesture can still be interpreted allegorically: the Old Testament is broken upon contact with the New, as is the case with the breaking spear in the crucifixion scene in the Uta evangelistary (see Chapter 1).

But the meaning of the allegory changes with the environment and becomes ambiguous. In the missal of Noyon (Fig. 18) the same concept recurs in portraying the sacrifice of the mass: Synagoga, wearing a blindfold, thrusts her spear through the sacrificial lamb.[9] As she does so, her spear breaks and opens the wound from which Ecclesia receives the blood of the Redeemer in the chalice.

The medallion (Fig. 65) of the cross of Bury St. Edmunds[10] is closely related in theme to the illustration in the Noyon missal. The spirit of the cross, a work of the late twelfth century, mirrors the developments described previously (see Chapters 4, 9, and 12). Although Ecclesia herself does not appear (angels, patriarchs, prophets, and apostles take her place as in medieval prophet plays), the cross is nevertheless a veritable compendium of the disputation between Ecclesia and Synagoga during the Middle Ages. As she pierces the lamb with her spear, Synagoga is confronted by the other figures, who accusingly hurl their testimonies at her.

The pointed hat quickly became the most common pictorial device for characterizing Jews.[11] Even Moses wears one in some depictions (in the *Sci Vias Domini* of Hildegard of Bingen, ca. 1175) as does Aaron, in whose arms Synagoga collapses after her dispute with Ecclesia (window in Le Mans, Fig. 19). In the antiphonary of St. Peter in Salzburg[12] (ca. 1150), the Roman soldiers who led Christ to the crucifixion are replaced by medieval Jews with pointed hats—a substitution reminiscent of the passion plays (cf. Chapter 12). The Master of Naumburg used the pointed hat for the high priests, body guards, and malicious counselors of Pontius Pilate. In the imaginative art of this master, this emblem loses its one-sidedness and is embedded in a larger context in which the entire doctrine of salvation can still be seen. But in the widely circulated miniatures and in the arts and crafts, the delicate and complicated theme of Ecclesia and Synagoga is severed from the original context of the doctrine of salvation: the meaning of the Jew's hat and the instruments of torture has been intensified to the statement that medieval Jewry belonged with the murderers of Christ.

In the former convent of Wilten in Tyrol there was a silver paten and chalice (ca. 1160; today in Vienna) depicting, in splendid gold and silver work, the crucifixion together with Mary and John and the four Gospel symbols. On the flat rim of the dish (Fig. 21) is a highly wrought portrayal of Christ freeing the patriarchs from purgatory, while on the other side a group of nine Jews is approaching the flaming door of hell. The leader of the group carries a banderole with the name SINAGOGA; the last figure looks back wistfully at the door to paradise, which is closed and guarded by angels. The inscription on the outer rim reads: "*Que reprobat Christum / Synagoga meretur abissum. Ecclesie fidei / dat gracia gaudia celi*" (Synagoga, since she rejects Christianity, deserves the abyss of hell. God's grace bestows heavenly joys on the loyal Ecclesia). The inscription on the chalice reads: "*In Testamento veteri / quasi sub tegumento / Clausa latet nova lex / novus in cruce quam reserat rex*" (In the Old Testament, just as under a cover, the New Covenant is concealed, which the new King unsealed on the cross).

This portrayal might still be interpreted symbolically. The paten is devoted to the Easter events; Christ's descent to hell is part of the Christian tradition. The scene at the gate of hell might be explained by Matthew 25:41—"Depart from me, you cursed, into the eternal fire prepared for the devil and his angels"—a passage that even earlier was related to Synagoga and is found, for example, on the Gunhilda cross in Copenhagen (cf. Chapter 1). There, however, this curse refers to sinful man as such; here it is aimed directly at medieval Jewry, and a purely symbolic interpretation is hardly possible any longer. The hatred of the Jews, which was a product of the times, intruded into the portrayal whose original theological message is so clearly formulated in the inscription on the chalice. Perhaps, too, the anger is expressed at the resistance that the Jews generally offered to the attempts to convert them.[13] The symbol has become ambiguous and engenders its own hate-filled reality.

In other portrayals, the devil in the form of a serpent coils itself around Synagoga's head, covering her eyes—as earlier on the main portal of Notre Dame de Paris, built in the reign of Philip Augustus, who drove the Jews out of France. A similar representation is found in the illustrated Bible of Petris de Funes, dating from 1197 (Bibliothèque Municipale, Amiens; Fig. 22).[14] Sometimes a purse also hangs from Synagoga's waistband symbolizing avarice and usury, and perhaps the thirty pieces of silver. In the passion window of the cathedral in Chartres (between 1215 and 1240) a devil shoots an arrow into Synagoga's eye (Fig. 20). The symbol of the veil is thereby forsaken: eternal blindness takes the place of the veil which might still be removed.

Occasionally it is an angel that metes out retribution to Synagoga; on the west portal of St. Gilles (largely destroyed) the angel knocked the crown from her head and threw her to the ground. On a bronze relief of the descent from the cross by Benedetto Antelami in Parma (late twelfth century), an angel rushes down upon Synagoga and throws her to the ground, while another angel leads Ecclesia to the Lord.

It is certain that such scenes developed in connection with the passion plays. The characters in the scenes on pulpits fashioned by Nicolo and Giovanni Pisano (in Pisa, Siena, and Pistoja) appear as if crowded together on a small stage and arranged with regard to their scenic effect. The sculptor composes, and his poetic treatment of the religious symbols is at once pursued by the imagination of the viewer.[15] "A Jew [below the cross] strokes his curly beard with one hand and with the other pulls back the folds of his clothing in order blasphemously to expectorate" (Battisterio, Pisa). "But terror lays hold of the assembled Jews. As if driven by a storm, they rush out, looking around in fear and trembling while falling over one another or cowering on the ground in an attempt to escape" (Pistoja). "The Jews cringe into the cowls of their robes and look around fearfully; however, they appear to have stones ready to throw or to be just picking them up" (Siena).

On the crown of the altar in the church of St. Mary on the Meadow in Soest, dating from the early thirteenth century, three scenes from the passion play are depicted: Christ before Caiaphas, the crucifixion with Ecclesia and Synagoga, and the women at the tomb. In the crucifixion scene an angel pushes Synagoga away from the cross with a lance, while on the opposite side Ecclesia holding the chalice is led to Christ (Fig. 23).

III

Another group of pictorial representations goes back to the disputation between Ecclesia and Synagoga. The *disputatio* was first enacted at the foot of the cross, but in connection with the ecclesiastical dramas developed into an independent scene. It is the most common motif within the theme of Ecclesia and Synagoga and the one most fraught with consequences; it concentrates the religious conflict in two characters, separates this conflict from other motifs, and prepares the two adversaries for their appearance in portal sculpture, where the theological argumentation moves into the area of human experience and intensifies into emotional expression.

What is apparently the earliest example of the *disputatio* is found on a book cover from Hildesheim (today in Trier; Goldschmidt III, 55; Fig. 24), about 1170, soon after the *Ludus*. Ecclesia appears at the foot of the cross in her traditional form with crown, chalice, banner, and halo. Synagoga is leaving the scene with a gesture of protest; the crown has fallen from her head and her eyes are blindfolded; in her left hand she holds the unbroken spear. In addition to this traditional arrangement, the two women appear a second time in the wide border of the book cover, considerably enlarged and independent of the central scene: Ecclesia is clothed as if for a tournament with shield, helmet, and banner; Synagoga retreats, carrying the knife of circumcision over her shoulder like a sword.

This conception must have been wide-spread, for on a semicircular enamel tablet in the Museum Cluny in Paris,[16] the *disputatio* at the foot of the cross is reproduced precisely and the figures explained in succession from left to right: "*Hec parit*" (this one gives birth; Mary), "*Hec credit*" (this one believes; Ecclesia), "*Obit hic*" (this one dies; Christ), "*Fugit hec*" (this one flees; Synagoga), and "*Hic obedit*" (this one obeys; John). The conflict is reduced to a simple formula in *credit* and *fugit*—on the Hildesheim book cover it is "*surgit*" (she arises; Ecclesia) and "*cadit*" (She falls; Synagoga)—and at the same time expanded beyond the narrow framework of the *disputatio*.

In the illustration from Paderborn [17] (Fig. 25) the crucifixion and *unio mystica* are still dominant, but the two women have become more lifelike.[18] Ecclesia the queen is more stable and more concisely sketched than the figure of Synagoga, whose statuesque security is endangered by the richly flowing garment. What is later found fully developed in Bamberg and

Strasbourg as a three-dimensional corporeal motif is heralded here in muted tones in two-dimensional form. The narrow blindfold of Synagoga appears here in the same form as it does later in Bamberg. The four half-length pictures of the prophets are reminiscent of the prophet play and testify to the coming fusion of the *Ordo Prophetarum* and the two female figures. The disputation is concentrated in the banderoles: "*Dilectus meus candidus et rubicundus*" (My beloved is all radiant and ruddy; Song of Solomon 5:10) refers to the crucified Lord. Synagoga quotes a line from Deuteronomy 21:23, which refers to the punishment for disobedient sons: "*Maledictus qui pendet in lingno*" (a hanged man is accursed by God). Thus, again Synagoga appears in the role of the mother of Christ, who is the disobedient son to whom that curse applies.

Such portrayals correspond very closely to the conception of Albertus Magnus. In his commentary on the Sacrament of Holy Communion, he describes Ecclesia and Synagoga as follows:

> To the right of the Crucified a maiden is portrayed with a joyful expression and beautiful face and crown; it is Ecclesia, who reverently receives the blood of Christ in the chalice . . . whereas on the left stands a figure with eyes blindfolded, a sad expression and bowed head from which the crown falls; it is Synagoga, who has spilled this same blood and still despises it.[19]

The *disputatio* had become separated from the crucifixion. In a window in Le Mans, St. Peter crowns Ecclesia after her victory and Aaron holds Synagoga, who is collapsing in his arms (Fig. 19). In a window in Chartres (Fig. 20), both figures appear with the same symbols they presumably were identified with in processions and pageants: Ecclesia with standard and cross, crown and halo, the tree of life, and a model of a church in her right arm. Synagoga's standard is bent, in her left hand she holds the crown which has fallen from her head, and her eyes are blindfolded. The devil shooting an arrow is probably taken from a scene in a pageant. The initial *T* (Fig. 27) from a fourteenth-century manuscript repeats details of the window in Chartres in the grouping that had become customary since the thirteenth-century statuary.

There are, at the same time, other variants of the *disputatio*: in Monreale, Ecclesia crowns a king while Synagoga, surrounded by Jews, stands off at one side in shackles. On the south portal of the cathedral in Chartres, St. Jerome takes a scroll from Synagoga [20] which denotes first of all, in the literal sense, the translation of the Old Testament into Latin. In the Salzburg Antiphonary (twelfth century), Synagoga wears a yoke as a symbol of her being bound to the old law; she goes forth on an ass to meet Ecclesia who rides proudly on horseback, as appeared later in the Tucher window in the Freiburg Cathedral (Fig. 28). The *disputatio* has become a tournament in the dress of the chivalric era: Synagoga rides forth into the one-sided contest in her yellow dress, with blindfolded eyes and a broken lance, on a limping ass. Her most distinctive emblem is the goat's head, which in the era about 1300 no longer signified the sacrificial animal of the Old Testament, but rather unchastity—in the narthex of the Freiburg Cathedral it is the emblem for lust (Luxuria; Fig. 40).

IV

Common to the two groups of motifs that have been discussed so far is the fact that abstract Christian dogma was translated into the ideas, language, and conflicts of the contemporary world. In the first instance, the judgment and vengeance of man usurped the position of divine judgment; in the second, the spiritual content was translated into the temperament of the times—the gestures, costumes, and dialect of the people. The symbolism of the figures thereby became more realistic, leading to the identification of all Jews with the "murderers of Christ."

Opposing these tendencies was the eschatological tradition underlying the teachings of Bernard of Clairvaux, Suger of St. Denis, the *Ludus de Antichristo*, and the stained-glass work of the twelfth and thirteenth centuries. In these the complex doctrine of *Concordia*, together with the successive stages of revelation, was fully developed and portrayed.

The famous window in the abbey church of St. Denis (Fig. 31) stands at the beginning of this series and largely determined it. The design for this window is traditionally ascribed to the learned abbot and statesman Suger, who died in 1151. He was a contemporary of Bernard of Clairvaux and the *Ludus* poet, and in the construction of his abbey church he laid the groundwork for the emergence of the Gothic cathedrals.[21] Ideas relating to the mysticism of Bernard of Clairvaux were formulated here for the first time. Therefore, it is not surprising that the *Concordia* appears here in a clear, effective artistic form.

In the uppermost of the five large medallions in the window stands Christ as a king dispensing justice, his body and arms forming a cross, exalted above grief and pain, hatred and joy. "With his right hand he crowns Ecclesia and with his left removes the blindfold covering Synagoga's face. What else can this allegory stand for but the arrival of the New Covenant in the world and its proclamation? Christ uncovers the secret of the Old Covenant which was veiled, so to speak, behind a blindfold." [22] This idea is emphasized by the colors: Ecclesia's mantle is green, Synagoga's rust-red; both colors appear on Christ—on his undergarment and his mantle. Synagoga holds a hyssop branch, the sign of atonement and purification (cf. Chapter 1). Her face is uncovered, she wears the clerical robe, and carries the tablets of the law in her hands.

In the second medallion Moses and Christ stand side by side. Moses's head is covered with the veil that was intended to conceal his transfigured contenance from the people. Christ raises his right hand and removes the veil, as St. Paul states in II Corinthians 3:14. This was the actual biblical origin of the veil motif. Again, greens and reds appear around the two figures. The banderole reads: "*Quod Moyses velat / Christi doctrina revelat / Denudant Legem / Qui spoliant Moysem*" (What Moses conceals / is revealed by the teachings of Christ / who removes the veil from the law / and lifts the veil of Moses).

The *Concordia* doctrine continues to be represented in the three other medallions: in the third we see the "mystic mill" to which the grain sacks of the Old Testament are carried. St. Paul turns the mill, from which the fine flour of the New Testament pours forth. In another medallion the cross grows out of the Ark of the Covenant.

In the window in the abbey church of St. Denis, as in the

Ludus, Synagoga wears a blindfold that is to be lifted on judgment day. Both works, created at about the same time, give the eschatological answer to the religious conflict; both are rooted in the mystical teachings of Bernard of Clairvaux.[23]

At this point the question of the time of origin of the veil motif can be phrased more precisely. We have attempted to explain the dissemination of this new motif from the *Ludus de Antichristo* (pp. 90–91) and from the conciliatory words of St. Bernard, "Yet in the evening they will repent, and then their reward will not be wanting" (p. 74)—which seems like a softening of strict dogmatism pointing directly to the Bamberg figures. The contemporaneity of the *Ludus* with Suger's window in the abbey church of St. Denis is obvious. But the question still remains of how an event, which probably occured only once—namely, the production of the *Ludus* at the court of Barbarossa—and in surroundings somewhat hostile to the church, could have brought about such profound enrichment in the figure of Synagoga far beyond national boundaries. It seems likely that this new development in the motif was aided by other more profoundly influential ideas that made the veil motif dominant for an entire century. This writer believes that the additional forces are to be found in the environment, teachings, and artistic views of Suger of St. Denis.[24]

Suger had risen to positions of high ecclesiastical and diplomatic honor early in life; during his absence on a mission to Rome his monks elected him abbot. Thereby, he reached a position that permitted him to give free reign to his talents, ambitions, and vision. The abbey church of St. Denis was the shrine of the patron saint of France and the final resting place of French kings. During his relatively short life Suger succeeded, through his tireless efforts and breadth of vision, in making St. Denis the political and religious center of France. He devoted all his efforts to the preparation of the Second Crusade in 1147. Louis VII, who took part in the crusade himself, made Suger regent of France. In the rebuilding of the abbey church of St. Denis during the last decade of his life, Suger finally found himself in a position to give full expression to his political, religious, and artistic ideas.

We may turn therefore to Suger's view of art. The portal of the cathedral was for him the entrance in both the natural and the symbolic sense. It was designed as the gate of heaven. This is an example of the anagogical element in Christian art—that is, that through art the human spirit is led to ineffable truths. Thus Suger's Neoplatonic view of art coincided with the teachings of his contemporary, Bernard of Clairvaux. This view held that religious art was permissable insofar as it was able to lead the viewer to the eternal source of beauty—that is, in its anagogical function. The viewer was admonished not to spend time in admiring the material value and splendor of the work, but to rise up "to the true light . . . to which Christ is the portal"; in this way the mind rises above the sensual world that holds it captive. Thus the *analogous* character of beauty (i.e., the part it has in a transcendental ideal) is realized along with the *anagogical* function of art (to prepare the mind for the understanding of ultimate truths).

To demonstrate these two functions in the new architecture of which Suger dreamed, we must consider the power and the role of light, its freedom of movement around the columns supporting the vault, and its distribution at various times of day. Suger understood "light" in its literal and physical sense as well as in its analogical and anagogical sense. Light was the basic metaphysical experience in his religion and art. In this respect the chancel of the abbey church of St. Denis with its five-part vault achieves faultless perfection and complete expressiveness. One could almost say that Suger was "intoxicated with light" (licht-trunken—as in Simson, p. 169) and that the relationship produced by light between brightness and obscurity, revelation and mystery was a central experience for him. He himself said that the "windows arrayed with sacred symbols" seemed to him like veils that at the same time conceal and reveal the ineffable. Indeed, the entire cosmos is the veil that is penetrated by divine light. This essential identity of his religion and his art becomes convincingly clear in the selection of iconographic figures that he identified with revelation and mystery, brightness and obscurity: he chose for his purpose the characters of Ecclesia and Synagoga, which were at that time approximately 1,000 years old and were about to enter their last and greatest stage through Suger's metaphysics of light. Suger was the one who led Synagoga out of the ghetto and back into the Christian community. In so doing he bestowed upon her once more the equality in position without which the high rank occupied by the two figures from then on would be inconceivable.

It is clearly evident that such a scheme must have derived from a specific metaphysical system and that this system was of decisive influence on the creative process. The source of this metaphysics is to be found in teachings and writings that were often commented upon in the Middle Ages and attributed to Dionysius the Areopagite, an Athenian converted by Paul (Acts 17:34) and regarded "as the first after the Apostles." Tradition made him the apostle of the French and author of the Areopagitic Writings. In the ninth century John Scotus Erigena, perhaps the most brilliant thinker of his time, undertook a new commentary commissioned by the emperor. On the basis of the Areopagitic Writings he set up his own metaphysical system. The metaphysics of Suger and the schools of architecture influenced by him were based on this system.

What connects that metaphysical vision with the architecture of the abbey church of St. Denis? It succeeds in constantly presenting the light as a life-giving, artistically creative, and ultimately divine quality. A stream of homogeneous light floods the chancel and spreads unhindered throughout the entire surrounding area. In the ecstatic yet so precise description of Suger, "the entire sanctuary is illuminated with a wondrous uninterrupted light which comes in through the most sacred windows"—namely, through Suger's famous window portraying Christ, Ecclesia, and Synagoga. The constantly effective and active experience of obscurity and brightness, mystery and revelation is entrusted not only to the columns and dome but also to the allegorical figures in which the words of sacred tradition are made visible.

The picture that Suger chose—namely, the pair Ecclesia and Synagoga—became identical with the fundamental religious experience of light in Suger's system. The two acquired a new impressiveness and a position on which the venerable *Concordia* of old could return. For wherever the two allegories appear in the windows of gothic cathedrals from that time on—even though engaged in the act of *disputatio* and displaying all their historic emblems—they appear in strict symmetry. Both women are queens and wear magnificent and, frequently, similar garments. The artistic equality of Synagoga is never called into question. Both again became members of a higher unity, the active experience of obscurity and brightness, mystery and revelation. Both have been elevated to the highest and most meaningful symbols of the Dionysian metaphysics of light. A white hood—a part of the tunic—often covers the head of Ecclesia as well, and at times is drawn lightly over the eyes of Synagoga as a mere intimation of her "blindness" while allowing freedom of sight to one eye. (cf. Figs. 26 and 29). The profound alternation between disguise and revelation—*velum* and *revelatio*—which was linked with the figure of Synagoga from the outset, is pursued here with the highest artistic virtuosity.

V

The disputation between the two women appears also in didactic art, as for example in the *Hortus Deliciarum*, which originated between 1160 and 1175 in the Hohenburg Convent in Alsace under the supervision of the learned abbess Herrad of Landsberg. The *Hortus* was an encyclopedia for the instruction of nuns and contained much that was worth knowing for them, above all, naturally, the divine plan of salvation. The figure of the Old Testament appears here as a rose window. The heads of Moses and Christ grow out of the same body. The banderole reads: "*Vetus et Novum Testamentum in simul junctum*" (Old and New Testaments combined in one). The New Testament is similarly depicted: Christ raises the chalice, which contains his own blood, and thus takes the place of the Old Testament sacrifice—"*Sit victima vera sacerdos*" (Let the priest be the true sacrificial lamb). The figures beneath the cross are furnished with symbols and banderoles: Ecclesia rides her tetramorph, and Synagoga rides an ass that has thrown off its yoke.

The *Hortus Deliciarum* had a great influence on medieval iconography. The two rose windows on the south side of the transept in Strasbourg (not yet replaced since the war) show the two phases of preparation and fulfillment symbolized by Synagoga and Ecclesia. The joust between the two women depicted in the Tucher window in Freiburg (Fig. 28) also seems to have originated in the *Hortus*, and even in courtly literature of the classical medieval period there are traces of it. In the *Younger Titurel* of Albrecht von Scharfenberg (ca. 1270) there is the following precise description of Ecclesia on her tetramorph:[25]

> A man, the image of a calf, a lion and an eagle,
> quite tame and in no wise wild, they safely bear Ecclesia,
> as she receives the wellspring of all fountains,[26]
> the source borne for our sake by this fair woman
> whom we behold clothed with the sun.

Here again we find a translation of the conflict into the spirit of the age—this time the world of knighthood and nobility—which we have often encountered.

The list of variants of our theme could be expanded, but we conclude this phase of development with an example presaging the commercial art of the late Middle Ages. From an ivory workshop in Soissons of the late thirteenth century come several small and quite similar two- and three-part portable altars on which Christ's passion is shown in a series of carvings.[27] Our two allegories appear here in the garb and with the gestures of the great portal statuary, but with their positions reversed: Ecclesia appears by the descent from the cross, and Synagoga at Christ's burial. The carvers evidently made use of certain proven models without being aware of the identity of the two allegories; in addition, the inconclusiveness of silent scenes may have contributed to the confusion of the symbols.

We have thus arrived at the era of great sculpture, indeed have gone beyond it in some respects, and so turn to it now.

Chapter 10

Symbols of Harmony

Just as Nature in manifold forms
Reveals One *God only,*
So, too, in the broad fields of Art
Is One *Eternal Spirit stirring:*
It is the spirit of Truth
Adorned in Beauty's *garb*
And confidently foreseeing
The brightest brilliance of the yonder Day.
—GOETHE

I

Bernard of Clairvaux had begun the process of refining the symbols of Ecclesia and Synagoga, purifying them from the polemics of the times; Suger of St. Denis had put them into artistic form. This prepared the theme for its incorporation into monumental statuary.

During the twelfth century the Gothic cathedral had come into being in France and had developed into an extensive architectural system—an enormous representation of the anticipation of divine grace. The positioning of the statuary on the portals, the "gates to the heavenly city," had an important part in this representation. On the tympanum, at the threshhold between the profane world and the splendor of God, appears the depiction of the last judgment, the crucifixion, and the crowning of Mary; here the visitor comes face to face with the protagonists of the Judeo-Christian tradition, the kings and prophets, the apostles and saints. The witnesses of the Old and New Covenants are brought together; here, too, Ecclesia and Synagoga appear. They are found at the entrances to the cathedrals in Bamberg, Strasbourg, Freiburg, Trier, and Magdeburg, among others. In some cases the original arrangement of figures was changed, in others it was left incomplete.

With the development of the cathedral, figural statuary was freed from the columnar severity that, as on the west portal in Chartres, made it a rigid architectural element. The human body began to be perceived organically and set into motion; the infinitely varied and expressive interplay between body and garment—the movement of the body and the movement of the folds—now began. With the freeing of the body and its increasing independence from the wall (to which it nevertheless remained structurally related), with its mobility and plastic mass, symbolic physiognomy was replaced by human expression. All this took place in the measured "classical" framework in a rare balance between realism and inward greatness. This balance lets us view the figures in their human dimensions while at the same time portraying them as members of a higher order.

In this stage in the evolution of plastic art, which will be discussed here only in broad outline, one of the greatest sculptors of all time, the Master of Bamberg, took up the purified theme of Ecclesia and Synagoga.

That "incredible stroke of luck"—as Theodor Haecker defines classical art—occurred, "namely, the most intimate contact of a great creative potential and a great subject, so that each is worthy of the other . . ."; indeed, the greatest subject "given to the men of the time, even if only to an élite among them." [1]

As in every work of classical greatness, different motifs are combined in each of the two Bamberg figures. Underlying them is the motif of the disputation, but the scene is devoted to a dignified representation of the two related women and their different destinies.

Ecclesia and Synagoga in the Bamberg Cathedral (Figs. 32–4) stand out from the wall as fully developed statues. Their bodies arch forward energetically, yet remain bound to the wall. The two women are related not only externally by size and position, but also in the noble origin common to both: this is the ideal image of the courtly lady of that age, shaped artistically in a manner worthy of the subject. But it is precisely in this statuary motif, in the fascinating dialog between body and garment, that the differing messages of the two can be found.

Ecclesia's mantle surrounds her like an opened shell. Its sweeping yet richly differentiated folds and perpendicular lateral contours lend stability to the figure, emphasize the steadiness of the supporting leg, and cause the delicately figured upper part of the body to appear as if on a pedestal. The body does not stand rigid, but seems to move and lean somewhat to one side; nevertheless, it is firmly contained by the strict frontal position of the head and the repeatedly stressed perpendiculars. The characterization as Ecclesia is inferred neither from a banderole nor a triumphant gesture, but from her unshakable stance.

The youthful figure of Synagoga, which is not clothed in a mantle, is also constructed so that it "stands." But the balance is disturbed by the curved motifs to such an extent that the figure seems to sway from its pedestal. Whereas, in the case of Ecclesia, the turning of the upper part of the body is absorbed and equalized by the counter-movement of the mantle and the vertical axis of the head, this turning is, in Synagoga's case, carried further in the tilted head and in the two deep diagonal folds of the garment, so that the vertical component seems to become doubtful behind the curve that arches from head to toe. This wavering is thus not a snapshot of a fleeting moment but a compressing into lasting form of the phases of motion between standing and falling.

Every detail in the two statues is devoted to this contrast. Corresponding to Ecclesia's resolute gestures are Synagoga's weak, dangling arms; the ascending rhythm in the mantle of one figure is a counterpoise to the falling rhythm in the garment of the other. Whereas Ecclesia's head is enhanced by the crown and rendered complete in a formal sense, Synagoga's blindfold has a constricting effect that disturbs the formal harmony. Thus, in both content and form the given attributes heighten the significance of the figures. Synagoga's lance breaks at the same point where her hip buckles, and the tablets of the law slip from her limp left hand, emphasizing her weakness.

This statuary contrast is surpassed by the spiritual expression. Ecclesia is older and more mature, and her gaze is firm and clear. She appears with the dignity and solemnity of a reigning goddess. Synagoga, in contrast, is more youthful, desultory, vital, tender, and graceful; her body seems to have shot up in comparison with her sedate counterpart. The sinew-like folds are stretched more tightly and less intricately over the body, which is clearly detectable behind them. Through their energy they give the body the twisting movement that causes it to fall. Synagoga is more flesh and blood; she is more nature than spirit.

Thus, the sympathies of the Master and of the viewer are with her also. In her more strongly emphasized corporeality, she is the one who is endangered, a figure of tragic proportions. This intensification of the tragic theme—the proximity of beauty and disaster—is also in the nature of classical art.

The Bamberg Master enlarged the old theme by the additional contrast of earthly blindness and spiritual assurance; he internalized the tension by the confrontation of transitoriness and permanence, and thereby presented the two women on the basis of general human experience. And yet they are two sisters, physically and spiritually, as taught by St. Augustine and Origen. They are descended from the same noble line, the same house, but their life histories are different. Synagoga with her callow beauty and blindness must withdraw before she reaches maturity; this increases our sympathy with her tragic role. She does not acchieve the firmness and spiritual maturity of Ecclesia, who has surmounted the earlier stage through the encounter with Christ and now gazes imperturbably beyond the day of judgment.

Thus, the contending pair have become members of a higher order, related like light and shadow in Suger's metaphysics. Ecclesia represents redemption by the spirit, Synagoga the yet unredeemed, half-concealed nature of creation—a nature with which the artist himself felt identified.

He attempted the apparently impossible: he translated the Dionysian tradition of light—brightness and shadow, revelation and mystery—into the stony language of monumental statuary. The blindfold of his Synagoga is a mere film of gauze, which the full revelation can penetrate when the hour has come. The so bewildering and so promising play of the eyes in the colorful and magnificent stained-glass representations of

Synagoga—especially in Marburg (Fig. 29)—has its equally brilliant and masterful counterpart in stone at approximately the same time or barely a generation later.

The portal for which Ecclesia and Synagoga were intended was never constructed. For centuries they stood on either side of the "Prince's Portal," in front of the enormous buttress that dominates the north side and also the square before it. This was a suitable place for the figures, since they are thematically related to matters of eschatological significance, which are portrayed on the tympanum of the portal. This relationship was stressed by the pedestals on which they were placed: Ecclesia's depicting the Gospel symbols and a seated prophet, and Synagoga's showing a Jew whose eye is being bored out by a devil. This was, of course, neither the hand nor the spirit of the Master, but that of a later generation in which the polemic again found expression.

Since the year 1938 both figures have been installed in the interior of the cathedral in the south aisle. They now stand beside the columns flanking the choir-rail with the reliefs of disputing prophets and apostles.

II

What was spared by the iconoclasts, during the French Revolution, in the interior and on the south side of the transept in Strasbourg is of the highest artistic quality; the "Death of Mary," the statues at the "Angel's Pillar," some heads of the apostles, and the figures of Ecclesia and Synagoga. All of these are the work of the same artist and came only a few years after the statues in Bamberg.

Replicas of Ecclesia and Synagoga still stand in the original location on both sides of the double portal.[2] They are facing each other but are separated by the full width of the portal. The *disputatio* is more strongly emphasized than in Bamberg; the arrangement seems more dramatic (Figs. 35–7).

Ecclesia turns and gazes at Synagoga who, stung by her words, seems to totter. The two women are not represented in classic repose as in Bamberg but in a more dramatic position, which naturally also allows them to stand on their own. With increasing fluidity of movement the contrast between the two women becomes clearer. Overtones of the row of vertical columns are found in the vertical shaft of the standard of the cross. The long folds in Ecclesia's garment are variations on the vertical motif. Ecclesia supports herself on the shaft of her standard so that the figure seems to be in equilibrium; the position of the legs is concealed. Opposite her, Synagoga turns sharply and seems to be falling out of the composition on the portal. Her head with the blindfold is bowed, the flagstaff is broken in three places, and the entire figure is pointed downward, so to speak. Whereas the width of the top portion of her body is accentuated, the plastic volume toward the bottom is reduced by the deeply indented folds of her garment, so that the slender, lightly veiled standing leg becomes visible as the only support for the body. The somewhat austere beauty of the Bamberg figures has given way to a gentle elegance; the figure and its garment interact with the utmost subtlety.

Ecclesia and Synagoga are no longer the two sisters: the victorious queen gazes at her vanquished adversary, in whom the tragedy of unfulfilled expectation is expressed in even more human terms than in Bamberg. Meekly, Synagoga submits to the mystery of her fate, prepared for exile. Her blindness is without polemical characteristics; in the very moment of defeat her beauty is revealed.

About the turn of the nineteenth century—when the profound art of medieval masters was studied by scholars but largely neglected by the German public—it was a poet who, in viewing the figures in Strasbourg, felt and expressed the mysterious interrelation of religion and art, tragedy and beauty. These words were naturally lost in the tumult of the First World War. The first to speak of the "Strasbourg Sisters" [3] and to give them an interpretation similar to ours was Ernst Stadler: the Master had given "his deeply concealed life . . . to the defeated, outcast woman." Stadler concludes with these lines:

> That wondrously in divine surroundings
> Radiant with humility, her pure image may stand.

III

The universal idea underlying the systems of scholasticism revealed itself to the believer as divine love (*amor dei*) applied to the creation and redemption. To the thinker it appeared as the ordering principle (*ordo*) that develops from the divine nature and can be understood in stages by man. As beauty (*pulchritudo*) it inspired the observing and creating man who could make the right use of his senses.

The relationship of *amor dei*, *ordo*, and *pulchritudo* was proclaimed: a relationship in origin, goal, and essence, though the intensity was not always the same. With this came recognition of the relationship of all human endeavors that, whatever field they may be in, aspire to the divine order. No medieval thinker fulfilled this aspiration with greater persuasive force than Dante. This consummation of divine order enabled him to define the concept of the beautiful in political treatises and develop a system of ethics and politics in the form of great literature. The awareness came in stages, culminating in the revelation of the universal idea at the end of his pilgrimage: "the love that holds sun and stars in their courses" (*Paradiso* XXXIII, 145).

The only thing that can distort and possibly even obstruct this harmony of all human endeavors within the divine order is matter (*materia*), the element that the aspirations for divine order must overcome: inertia, indifference, and human weakness. The works of nature, like those of man, are imperfect (*Paradiso* XIII, 76–78):

> But nature produces only patchwork,
> Creates like a master who is indeed experienced
> In his art, yet with a trembling hand.

Centuries later in the sonnets of Michelangelo this tragic division of human endeavors was described in moving words and accepted as part of our destiny. Michelangelo's words hold the same persuasive power as Dante's. We are reminded of the stages of spiritual development in the Bamberg figures: Synagoga is the younger sister who must stop at a lower stage. Imperfection is her fate as it is of man in general.

Aesthetics, the study of the beautiful, was considerably more for the Middle Ages than just a classification of art genres, their methods, and expressive values; more than the study of contrast, proportion, composition, and color; and more than a classification of works of art. The medieval theory of art was directed at the nature, origin, and intent, that is, the stimulus and mission of the beautiful, and thus incorporated it into the *amor dei* and the *ordo*. Again it was Dante who considered this metaphysical service to be the mission of the beautiful: "to lead mankind back to the right way" (Convivio IV, i, 9).

The beautiful (*bellezza*) produces order and love progressively in the viewer, depending on the degree of perfection in form and the clarity of the message. *Bellezza* culminates in the transfiguration of the human countenance by love (*Paradiso* III, 58–60):

> Thereupon I to her: in thy eyes' light
> The wondrous, such a divine presence radiates
> Which transforms what was once thy face. . . .

The ideal of beauty, of which Synagoga had become unquestionably a part, placed her once more in the venerable thought system of *Concordia*. As long as the medieval masters granted artistic equality to this figure and sympathized with her fate, the idea of *Concordia* remained alive.

A later century, no longer aware of this idea, added a banderole to the Strasbourg figures, attempting to subordinate them to the prevailing orthodoxy. "With the blood of Christ I overcome thee," says Ecclesia; "the same blood blindeth me" is Synagoga's reply.

IV

The statues of Ecclesia and Synagoga at the Reims Cathedral are on a par with the Bamberg figures; here, too, Synagoga enjoys equal status under the aegis of *Concordia*. But the figures in Reims are also closely connected with the wording of the popular tradition: Synagoga's lips are contorted with pain—a concession to the liturgical processions and pageants.

Other early examples connect the two women with the old motif of the wise and the foolish virgins, for example, in Magdeburg (although there it was not the original intent), in Trier, and in Freiburg. This association is extremely interesting, since the symbolism shifted and the two figures lost the thematic independence and stature they had just regained. The connection with the wise and the foolish virgins occurred as far back as the *Hortus Deliciarum*. The virgins also belonged to the cycle of the last judgment: the parable concerns sudden and unexpected judgment and admonishes its hearers to be in constant readiness.

The virgins in the parable became popular through liturgical dramatizations and mystery plays. It was there that they were brought together with Ecclesia and Synagoga; the important change in the purport of the virgins, merely suggested by the parable, must have taken place there. The strict eschatological meaning of the parable was replaced by a popular, ethical interpretation—the wise virgins with their oil lamps became allegories of purity and chastity,[4] and the foolish virgins with their inverted jars of oil became allegories of frivolity and unchastity. Illicit love relationships and unbelief went hand in hand.[5] They are depicted in this fashion on the west portal of the Strasbourg Cathedral (Fig. 39). There the seducer, the "Prince of the World," stands at the head of the line of foolish virgins, with whom he is flirting. One of them is about to remove her outer garment. At the same time the wise virgins turn toward Christ.

This expanded interpretation of the parable was generally accepted. Like a sermon on the temptations of the flesh, the stony processions of virgins flank the church portals through which wedding parties passed (Bridal Portal).[6] The classical concept of Ecclesia and Synagoga did not permit this combination with the wise and the foolish virgins. In Strasbourg, the latter are depicted on the west portal, whereas Ecclesia and Synagoga are on the south side of the transept. Soon after, however, a concrete, more timely interpretation of the theme seemed more understandable and tempting and easier to sustain than the profound eschatological meaning. The two groups of virgins personified a contrast that seemed related to the one between Ecclesia and Synagoga after the latter two had been forced to give up their eschatological sense. Indeed, it is not uncommon to find an inverted chalice similar to an empty oil jar in the hand of Synagoga[7] (Fig. 38), while Ecclesia receives the blood of the Lord in her chalice.

Even in monumental statuary Ecclesia became the leader of the wise virgins and Synagoga the leader of the foolish ones. Visual and dramatic elements thereby again achieved predominance as did the older, more odious insinuations of immorality and adultery. It was an easy step to reinterpret Synagoga's decided corporeality (as in Bamberg and Strasbourg), her youthful beauty, and her grace simply as debauchery. Thus another, previously mentioned misinterpretation could be carried over to Synagoga: in the company of the foolish virgins the goat's head in her hand took on irrevocably the connotation of unchastity. So complete was the fusion of the two systems that the goat's head was occasionally placed in the hands of the foolish virgins themselves. On the baptismal font of Hans Apengeter in the Marienkirche in Lübeck (dated 1337; Fig. 41) and on another font by the same master in Wismar, the foolish virgins carry not only their empty oil jars, but also Synagoga's banner with the broken staff and long-horned goats' heads; Synagoga herself no longer needed to appear. The wise virgins hold their burning oil lamps in readiness, but they also appear with flagstaffs and chalices. Commercial artisans did not take the trouble to differentiate the emblems clearly. Occasionally Ecclesia's chalice became a burning oil lamp, the emblem of the wise virgins (as, for example, in a frieze depicting the virgins on an embroidered antependium from Lower Saxony, mid-fourteenth century; now in Berlin), while the foolish virgins, in their desperation, would fling away what appears to us to be the chalice. In the fourteenth century, the later period of our theme, the various systems have completely merged with one another; never again would Synagoga be able to free herself from this popular confusion, which is revealed above all in the passion plays.

For a short while the tradition of *Concordia* in monumental statuary succeeded in ennobling even the combination of Synagoga and the foolish virgins. In Magdeburg, Ecclesia and Synagoga had been brought together on the "Wedding Portal" with the two groups of virgins in an elaborate and magnificent composition. Ecclesia and Synagoga were formed under the influence of the Bamberg figures and were not intended to appear with the virgins at first.

The sculptures in the narthex of the Freiburg Catherdral, dating from the early fourteenth century, deserve special attention. There Ecclesia and Synagoga, in a magnificent and brilliant composition, became members of a moral and religious didactic system.

The numerous figures stand as if in a procession on both sides of the narthex. They direct attention to the Madonna and Child at the central pillar of the portal and to the reliefs depicting biblical scenes on the tympanum. The theme of temptation and self-mastery is stated in the two texts that angels hold out to those entering: "*Nolite exire*" (Do not wish to leave the condition of grace); "*Vigilate et orate*" (Be watchful and pray, lest you fall into temptation).

The theme of temptation is in full development: on the left stands the "Prince of the World," as in Strasbourg a stylishly dressed young man, the tempter of innocence, with moneybag and a bouquet of flowers. His bare back is covered with toads and worms, the symbols of corruption (Fig. 40). Beside him stands "lust," a naked woman with a goatskin over her shoulders carrying a goat's head in front of her. The third figure is the warning angel with the banderole reading "*Ne intretis in tentationem*" (Do not fall into temptation). The procession continues with five typological figures representing faith, followed by the five wise virgins and the figure of Christ teaching. The theme is presented fully: it begins with the temptation of the flesh, continues in the conquering power of faith, and culminates in the group of wise virgins with Christ.

Just as polyphonous is the procession on the right side led by Catherine of Alexandria, patron saint of knowledge, and St. Margaret of Antioch, who tamed the dragon. They are followed by figures of the seven liberal arts, the humanistic elements in the doctrine of salvation. They form the preliminary stage to divine truth that overcomes the folly of the senses, personified in the five foolish virgins. The procession of foolish virgins ends with Synagoga, who stands directly opposite Ecclesia. In this elaborate composition the heroic stature of Ecclesia and Synagoga becomes lost, to be sure, but precisely through their participation in the intricate and didactic arrangement of figures, the two antagonistic images lose their polemical severity.

A work from the Pöhlde Monastery, dated 1284 (Fig. 42),[8] has come down to us from the twilight that is now settling over the clarity of *Concordia.* Ecclesia and Synagoga faced each other on the sides of a choir stall, but only Synagoga is preserved. Her crudely carved figure evokes distant memories of the lofty style of Bamberg and Strasbourg. But her face is frigid and her neck bent as inexorably as her flagstaff. She carries a strikingly large goat's head with beard and horns—by that time a symbol of unmistakable clarity.

Chapter 11

Ecclesia Universalis

Thou wast anticipated in the chaos
Before the light was ready for my call.
I had assigned to thee a place in time
Ere I created the impatient one.
—FRANZ WERFEL

I

Thus far we have stressed the antinomy between Ecclesia and Synagoga and have traced the continuance of this conflict in literature and art until it was reconciled in the great statuary of the thirteenth century. But the concept of Ecclesia contains yet other elements that lie beyond this historically and dogmatically defined dualism and that make up the universal character of the Judeo-Christian belief in God. In the first words of the Gospel According to St. John, this character was claimed by the young Christian sect—"In the beginning was the Word"—just as it had been proclaimed earlier in the figure of "wisdom" in the Old Testament Proverbs of Solomon. Logos, "the word," as well as the "wisdom" of Solomon's Proverbs is God's conceptual and creative quality, that which bestows existence, form, and direction on the world. These are two identical symbols of the divine name.

In Christian tradition Ecclesia was formed from the elements of the logos and eventually equated with it. Although there was a long previous history, the equation was completely realized in the great illustrated Bibles of the Middle Ages, which are discussed in the following sections of the chapter. Ecclesia had become a timeless, universal figure, present and active even in the beginning: she is the doctrine, the word, the thought of God himself. She thus became not just the principal coordinate in the typological system, but grew beyond it insofar as the dualism Ecclesia-Synagoga as a mere phase of God's revelation receded into the background. In the *Ecclesia aeterna* Synagoga is both overcome and preserved.

This development was well prepared in the Old Testament. The figure of wisdom had been similarly elevated to the throne (Proverbs 8:22 ff.). It was not only the cultivation of the pure life, but the highest quality of God himself, which was present even "at the beginning of his work, the first of his acts of old." Before creation, since the beginning of time "I was beside him, like a master workman; and I was daily his delight, rejoicing before him always. . . ." The same idea is expressed in the apocryphal book of "The Wisdom of Solomon":

For she is an initiate in the knowledge of God, and an associate in his works [8:4].

With thee is wisdom, who knows thy works and was present when thou didst make the world, and who understands what is pleasing in thy sight and what is right according to thy commandments. Send her forth from the holy heavens, and from the throne of thy glory send her, that she may be with me and toil, and that I may learn what is pleasing to thee [9:9 ff.].

This Old and New Testament parallel is continued into the next millennium. In the rabbinical commentaries of the Talmud period,[1] the torah is equated with the figure of wisdom. In this capacity the torah is not only the exact parallel to the Christian figure of Ecclesia, but probably her forerunner and model as well. "When a king builds his palace he does not do it with his own hands but through the skill of an architect. The architect, too, does not build just any way he pleases, but makes use of diagrams and ground plans to arrange the rooms and place the doors. Thus God consulted the torah and created the world. . . ." In the Talmud literature God appears with the torah in his hand; it is the ground plan of the world, God's textbook, timeless and existent from the beginning. "This goes so far that not only does Abraham make use of the torah before it was handed down—how else could he be a model of Jewish piety according to Talmudic understanding?—but even God himself learns from his torah." [2]

The temporal dimension is disregarded; its quantitative succession is replaced by a qualitative order. Both the torah and Ecclesia stand at the beginning of things as ordering principles. And indeed we see Ecclesia, in the late medieval illustrated Bibles, at the very creation of the world.

Some examples of this concept of Ecclesia in medieval Christian literature will be cited here. In the Early Middle High German "Lob Salomos," [3] the Queen of Sheba appears as a type of Ecclesia, showing again the very close relationship that at first existed between the Jewish and Christian tradition:

> This queen, as I understand,
> Represents Ecclesia.
> She is said to be his spouse
> In secret and in public.
> I gather that she is wedded to him
> In divine communion.
> In abundance of virtue
> She is said to be his equal,
> And will bear him children
> Whom we will call divine heirs. . . .

In "Das fließende Licht der Gottheit," Mechthild von Magdeburg, a contemporary of the Bamberg Master, describes a vision in which "holy Christianity" appeared to her:

> The most beautiful maiden ever seen, apart from our beloved lady St. Mary, yet a companion of hers . . . She carries in her outstretched hand a chalice of red wine from which she drinks in indescribable rapture . . . that is the blood of her eternal son which fills her heart so much that she gives us much good instruction. . . .

> From this maiden's heart
> I saw a flowing fountain spring.
> To it were carried heathen children
> Who were all leprous and blind.

Above this fountain stood a very godly man
. . . That was John the Baptist
He washed the children in the fountain
And they regained their sight and health completely.

Ecclesia, holding the chalice, appears as an allegory for the sacrifice of the mass and as a divine doctrine; combined with the vision of the *fons vitae*, the source of life, she points out the contrast between blindness and the regaining of vision, which suggests the relationship to Synagoga.

In the reformation era, when many ancient symbols were obscured, Ecclesia's love—the most intimate and mysterious of her elements—remained untouched. What Christ loves the Christian, too, can love, directly and without intermediate symbolism. Thus Martin Luther chose the form of a love song for his "Song of the Holy Christian Church";[4] the *unio mystica* had become a highly personal experience:

She is dear to me, the worthy maiden,
I cannot forget her.
Her gentility and her honor are praised,
She has taken possession of my heart.
I am much in love with her,
And if I should
Have great misfortune,
That will not matter,
She will repay me
With the love and loyalty,
Which she shows to me
And satisfy all my wants.

From the wide spectrum of literature concerning Ecclesia, first one, then the other element was taken into the plastic arts; the illustrated typological Bibles, finally, sought to take in the entire tradition in hundreds of pictures and illustrations. We therefore turn our attention to the pictures in which Ecclesia appears as a single figure set above, or removed from, the typological contrast. Depending on the particular significance of Ecclesia, these documents can be grouped in various ways: *Ecclesia universalis* or *aeterna*, *Ecclesia triumphans*, *Ecclesia orans*. A great wealth of variants, religious speculation, artistic invention, and personal interpretation is revealed.

II

In the midst of a still pagan world during its early centuries, Christianity was even more aware of its twofold origin than it was later. St. Augustine considered Judaism and paganism as the foundation walls of theology, which unite in Christ as the cornerstone.[5] In Ecclesia the Jewish-Christians (*Ecclesia ex circumcisione*) and the pagan-Christians (*Ecclesia ex gentibus*) grew together to form a single community [6] in which they had equal status. Christian doctrine arched over both the Old Testament and the moral and philosophical teachings of pagan antiquity. The "spiritual Jerusalem," as St. Augustine declared, had existed even in pre-Christian times and among other peoples. Ecclesia did not need to feel ashamed of either her pagan or her Jewish ancestry; *Concordia*, in the broadest sense, was able to develop freely. The older of the ivory tablets discussed in the first chapter are in this tradition: Synagoga is the forerunner, Ecclesia the fulfillment; each stands at her own particular stage of revelation as a member of a higher unity, the *Ecclesia universalis*.

This idea is so strong that in a series of portrayals the opposing figure of Synagoga is missing. Thus on an ivory casket in Braunschweig, Ecclesia appears alone, even though the work dates from the late Carolingian period and in composition and technique is closely related with the ivories from Metz.[7] In place of Synagoga, Stefaton appears, the soldier with the sponge of vinegar. In a remote village church in the Auvergne (Moissat-Bas, Puy-de-Dôme), there is a major work of twelfth-century goldsmithery, the shrine of St. Lomer, which originated in Limoges. Christ is depicted there as a judge in the midst of the saints. The main field portrays the crucifixion with Mary and John, while the outer fields are reserved for Ecclesia and the centurion (Fig. 43). In a window of the cathedral in Sens, dating from the late twelfth century, Synagoga's traditional place is taken by an archangel, who puts his sword of vengeance in its sheath as a sign that justice has been satisfied through the death of Christ.

This universal conception of Ecclesia avoided the dualism

of the *disputatio* and the risk of ambiguous symbols. *Ecclesia universalis*, the principal figure together with Christ, embraced the stages of earlier revelation. In the miniature on the title page of the Bernward Bible in Hildesheim (Fig. 44), Moses, holding the book of Genesis, walks up to a regal-looking woman who stretches her arms toward him: Ecclesia is taking the Old Testament into her safekeeping. In the illuminated typological Bibles that appeared during the classical period of the Middle Ages, Ecclesia frequently appears as the guardian of the treasure of the Old Testament.[8]

Within the *Ecclesia universalis*, the historical and political aspect of the salvation process was developed in the *Ecclesia triumphans*. Through the reforms of the Cluniac order the church had largely freed itself from secular control, the papal claims to authority grew steadily from the time of Gregory VII to that of Innocent III, and the armies of the crusades set forth under the spiritual leadership of the popes—a powerful expression of Christian unity.

On the portal of the abbey church of Vézelay in Burgundy (1125), this concept of dominion finds mystical and majestic expression: Christ in glory distributes the gifts of the Holy Ghost to the apostles. Within his all-embracing, life-giving arms appear the people of all times and all lands, all the crafts, and all the signs of the zodiac, while Peter and Paul, at the feet of Christ, proclaim and gather together the triumphant universal church. It was in this same city that Bernard of Clairvaux preached in the year 1146 before French knighthood and charged them to take up the cross; fifty years later, it was here that French and English knights and princes entered upon the Third Crusade. The *Ludus de Antichristo* (Chapter 8) should also be recalled.

Portrayals of the *Ecclesia triumphans* are found that date from the tenth century on. An early example is the sacramentary of Petershausen,[9] which originated on the island of Reichenau in Lake Constance: beside the *Majestas Domini* sits Ecclesia the Queen on her throne. She wears a crown and halo and holds a scepter and book but, significantly, no chalice.

Also dating from the era of Bernard and the *Ludus* is the ceiling painting in the church at Prüfening near Regensburg: a mighty, regal figure with a crown and the standard of the cross, holding a symbol of the world and a cross in her left hand. The *Ecclesia triumphans*, riding a tetramorph, appeared in the Worms cathedral in the thirteenth century. In a miniature dating from the second half of the thirteenth century (Rosenwald Collection, National Gallery of Art, Washington, D.C.), she is enthroned as ruler of the world together with Christ (Fig. 45; cf. also an ivory in the Hessisches Landesmuseum in Darmstadt showing the *Majestas Domini* with Ecclesia; also the initial *O*, Ecclesia on the throne, Codex Latinus 15701, folio 230, Staatsbibliothek, Munich).

The *Ecclesia orans*, lastly, appeared in the form of a woman praying or giving her blessing.[10] Her ancestress was the early Christian orant. She is found in the miniatures frequently as a protectress against temptations and the wiles of the devil and was carried over into the illuminated typological Bibles in this role.

III

The tradition of Ecclesia that lasted more than a thousand years finally had its fullest development in the illuminated Bibles of the thirteenth to fifteenth centuries. Every typological possibility was utilized in these Bibles. Personal speculations came to the fore along with the view accepted by the church; these illuminated Bibles were produced at the request of men of high station in the secular world and probably were not always subject to the approval of the clergy. Biblical typology, then fully developed, became engaged in the affairs of daily existence, the problems of life and death. The daily application and reappearance of the biblical types was observed and preached; the typology was transformed into an ever-watchful code of ethics. Popular beliefs and proverbs, virtues, suffering, and vices appeared in the framework of the doctrine of salvation and were classified, ranked, and judged in this context. Basic biblical truths and allegories, but also social classes were represented by established figures: God, angels, devils, Adam, Eve, Moses, the saints, knights, and noblewomen. Ecclesia usually appeared in the traditional manner with mantle, crown, chalice, and cross-staff; Synagoga with the tablets of the law and her veil (often merely suggested), with falling crown and breaking staff, from which a banner depicting a scorpion sometimes hangs.

Four illustrated Bibles that originated in France between 1230 and 1416 are of principal importance to our theme.

1. Bible moralisée (Codex Latinus 11560 of the Bibliothèque Nationale, Paris).[11] This part of an illustrated Bible from Job to Malachi contains short texts. Other parts of this Bible are in Oxford and London; complete copies are in Toledo (with a few pages in the Pierpont Morgan Library in New York) and in Vienna. It originated about 1230 and was later supplemented. Each of the 222 pages contains eight medallion-type miniatures.

2. Bible historiée toute figurée (Codex Fr. 9561, Bibliothèque Nationale, Paris).[12] About one hundred Old Testament events are depicted, furnished with a short text, and related to events in the New Testament. The Codex originated in the thirteenth and fourteenth centuries and was for a long time erroneously referred to as the Bible of Queen Jeanne d'Evreux.

3. Bible historiée (Codex Fr. 167, Bibliothèque Nationale, Paris).[13] This Bible, with text in Latin and French, originated about 1390 and was owned by Philip the Bold, the first Duke of Burgundy from the house of Valois. It is illustrated with four pairs of pictures on each page, arranged typologically. The Codex contains a total of well over 5,000 miniatures, many of high quality.

4. Bible historiée (Codex Fr. 166, Bibliothèque Nationale, Paris).[14] This is a typological Bible of the widest scope, illustrated by Paul of Limburg (the painter of the "Très Belles Heures du Duc de Berry") and his brothers for Philip of Burgundy and later for Jean de Berry. The work, begun in 1402, remained incomplete after the death of Berry in 1416. After page 47 the quality declines and many of the illustrations are mere sketches.

In Codices 9561, 167, and 166, Synagoga is sometimes used as a type in a surprisingly dramatic fashion, but in general appears infrequently. Codex 11560, the oldest of the four, reveals more of the tensions of the times. The contradictoriness and stubbornness of the Jews in resisting conversion are more often depicted: Jews who turn away from the preaching friars enter the jaws of hell; a Jew contradicts Ecclesia, who is attempting to enlighten him, and he is seized by the devil (both examples from the book of Psalms). Among the sinners whom Christ himself casts into hell are Jews with pointed hats (in the book of Isaiah). A Jew thrusts the spear into Jesus's side (book of Lamentations). All these scenes are within the framework of what has been hitherto discussed; they are not surprising in that they come from the century of the Fourth Lateran Council, the forced conversions, and the *Ecclesia triumphans.* What is surprising is how rare this allusion is in the more than 1,700 miniatures of Codex 11560. Also, one must not isolate the pictures from the pertinent biblical text that gives rise to them. Thus, in the Lamentations of Jeremiah, which played such an important part in the origin of the figure of Synagoga,[15] the grieving Queen of Zion, the ancestress of Synagoga, appears and bewails the fact that her children have been seized by devils. Or Synagoga stands by helplessly, as a devil leads away a group of sinners roped together. She is helpless and defeated, but never dishonored.

Several basic typological systems are common to these four Bibles—first of all the *Concordia Veteris et Novi Testamenti.* It is a principal concern of Codex 167 especially, where, for example, God appears in the burning bush (folio 20v.) between Ecclesia and Synagoga. The commentary is: "All who rightly understand the purpose and meaning of the Old Covenant will find that the Old Law and the New Law are but one and the same." This idea is illustrated over and over. In Ezekiel (folio 206) Christ appears on the cross with Ecclesia. Below them, in the old compositional symmetry, a Christian baptism is depicted on the left and an Old Testament sacrifice on the right, with an apostle and Moses standing by. On folio 200, Ecclesia hands the Ten Commandments to a bishop; on folio 115 she stands with Synagoga beside the Madonna and child. The death and burial of Moses are interpreted entirely in the spirit of *Concordia*, with both Synagoga and Ecclesia present (Codices 166 and 167, folio 46v.).

An important theme that presents itself to the viewer in a most striking fashion in the first pages of Codices 9561, 167, and 166 [16] is the mystical presence of Ecclesia at the creation (Fig. 47). This concept comes from both Old and New Testament sources, from the figure of wisdom, and from the logos of the Gospel According to St. John. Figure 47 (from Codex 9561, folio 3) shows this comprehensive, encoded composition in a magnificent design, the meaning of which is revealed both by the figures and by the scriptural passages. As God establishes the firmament, divides the land from the water, and molds the earth with his hands into an enormous sphere, Ecclesia is present, standing in her Gothic dwelling, surrounded by the green sea and shining gold sea monsters.

> The Lord created me at the beginning of his work, the first of his acts of old. Ages ago I was set up, at the first, before the beginning of the earth. When there were no depths I was brought forth . . . When he established the heavens, I was there, when he drew a circle on the face of the deep, when he made firm the skies above . . . then I was beside him . . . [Proverbs 8:22 ff.].

Ecclesia-Wisdom is not just a witness to the creation, but the divine inspiration itself. God studies the ground plan of the cosmos in the scroll that she lays before him—"I was beside him, like a master workman" (Proverbs 8:30). Both God the Creator and his wisdom are surrounded by the same colored circle of the universe.[17]

This composition is broadened in the two later codices (167 and 166); the separation of the light from the darkness is conceived and depicted typologically: the descent of the Holy Ghost signifies the creation of light. Defiant-looking Jews stand on the side of darkness, while Synagoga wavers undecidedly between the two groups (Codex 166, folio 1). The same situation recurs in the separation of the water from the dry land. Ecclesia-Wisdom stands on solid ground under her Gothic canopy while the *amaritudines mundi*, the bitterness of this world, surrounds her like waves lapping at her feet. Scenes of a martyr on the left and an amorous couple on the right illustrate the main point: suffering and passion have been reduced to a common denominator of bitterness and transitoriness (Codex 166, folio 1; Fig. 50).

Another great theme common to all four codices is the typological equating of Adam and Eve with Christ and Ecclesia, which goes back to St. Paul (Romans 5 and Ephesians

5:21 ff.). The relationship of Adam and Eve is transferred to Christ and the church. In this regard there is a highly concentrated, pictographic sort of composition in Codex 166 (folio 206), and a similar such one in Codex 11560 (folio 186; Fig. 49). In the foreground God takes Eve out of the side of the sleeping Adam while Moses and a prophet stand at His side. In the center Ecclesia comes out of the wound in the side of the crucified Lord; she is, like Eve, naked, but provided with a chalice, crown, and halo. On the left a monk lifts a child from the baptismal font. The accompanying text states: "As Eve was formed in Adam while he slept, so, too, was Ecclesia in Christ when he died on the cross. She was created through his sacred blood." In the later Codex 9561 this composition is further expanded: God unites the hands of Adam and Eve, and Christ is wedded to Ecclesia (Fig. 48).[18] In another miniature Ecclesia is betrothed by means of a ring to the Christ Child sitting on her knees. From the pictures and between the lines one reads a sermon on the sanctity of marriage.

The crucifixion, where Ecclesia originated, is thematically related to the *unio mystica*, Christ's choosing between Ecclesia and Synagoga. It is illustrated typologically by Jacob's choice between Rachel and Leah.[19] Christ places one hand on Ecclesia's shoulder while pushing Synagoga away with the other.[20] The *unio mystica* is pursued in St. John's apocalyptic vision of the New Jerusalem in Revelation 21 and 22. Ecclesia appears repeatedly at the side of the heavenly bridegroom "as a bride adorned for her husband. . . ." A good example is found in the pages in the Pierpont Morgan Library, related to the Codex 11560; in the Codex 167 (Fig. 51), Ecclesia and Christ share in the dangers and triumph of the apocalypse.

Of special interest, in view of the constant danger of isolating and misinterpreting symbols, are the portrayals of the death and burial of Synagoga found in Codices 9561, 166, and, in variants, 167 as well. After Moses, in his anger, has smashed to pieces the tablets of the law and holds aloft the new tablets (Codex 9561, folio 74v.), we see Synagoga, the typological counterpart, lying on the ground—an old woman dressed in black with torn banner and broken flagstaff. Christ and Ecclesia bend over the fallen woman solicitously. With one hand Christ points at Synagoga, and in the other he holds the book of the

New Covenant over her head with the same gesture as Moses, who is holding the tablets in the picture above.

The corresponding picture in Codex 166 (folio 44) shows Moses with the broken tablets in one hand and the new tablets in the other, while Synagoga lies on the ground and Ecclesia herself holds aloft the new tablets. The inscription reads: ". . . *lex judeis data illis nolentibus operari non permansit. Evangelium . . . gentibus datum est . . . ducat in saeculum . . .*" (The law that was given to the Jews, who would not fulfill it, was short-lived; but the Gospels, which are given to all peoples, will endure forever).

The above-mentioned miniature of the burial of Moses also belongs in this group. A new stage of revelation commences: the old tablets must be broken, Moses and Synagoga must die, and the law loses its force among the *judeis . . . nolentibus.* The promise of the New Covenant is, however, already contained in the Old: Christ and Ecclesia gaze down sympathetically at the dead Synagoga. The tablets of the law, a type of the gospels, pass into the hands of Ecclesia.

In Codex 166 (folio 40v.) the solemn burial of Synagoga is depicted in the same spirit (Fig. 52). She is being carefully placed in a sarcophagus by two evangelists, is mourned by the two others, wears a crown on her head, and holds the undamaged tablets of the law in her hands. At the foot of the sarcophagus Christ blesses the body; at the head, Ecclesia, who has been crowned as Synagoga's successor, looks down on the ceremony. The scene is interpreted typologically as the death of Miriam and her burial by Moses and Aaron. The meaning of this group is clear and in agreement with the others: Synagoga must die just as Miriam and Moses had to die in the wilderness before mankind could enter the Promised Land under Christ's leadership. The spirit of this portrayal is conciliatory; the doctrinal contradictions seem resolved in the successive stages of revelation ordained by God.

Another highly dramatic scene, which appears only in Codex 9561 (folio 89), ought to be included here: Synagoga, in a torn black mantle, has fallen to the ground; Christ stands behind her and is pointing at her. The text states that God has smitten her with *mesele*,[21] just as he had smitten Job and Poor Henry, and that for this reason Christ spurns her. The twelfth chapter of the book of Numbers is applied to Synagoga: Miriam, the type of Synagoga, is stricken with leprosy as punishment for her opposition to Moses, and is healed only after Aaron has interceded in her behalf.

Of the numerous other typological groups, just two will be mentioned: in Codex 9561 (folio 58) we see the paschal lamb that is sacrificed by the Jews before the Exodus, the blood of which is put on the lintel and doorposts to ward off the avenging angel. The lamb is the type of the crucifixion and the sacrifice of the mass: the priest raises the chalice to protect his congregation from diabolical demons. And in folio 2v. we see a female figure, blond and dressed in blue like Ecclesia, among the angels present at the creation. In her arm she carries a book with the symbol of Christ—a golden pentagram. The New Covenant is thus typologically present even on the first day of creation. God the Creator is connected with this figure by a scroll—a variation of the Ecclesia-Sapientia.

Each of these typological groups that have been discussed contains a parable, indeed, the quintessence of a sermon, and thus, as a Christian moral doctrine, becomes relevant to daily life. Every day stands under the judgment of God; Christ is the judge and Ecclesia the doctrine. Her omnipresence illuminates and determines every situation in life. She receives the soul of a friar on his deathbed, she succors dying martyrs, she inspires an apostle confronted by idol worshippers, she attends the confession of a young person who is being offered a potion by a devil, she presides at a dispute between Jews and their prophets, and she washes the feet of the poor. Above all—and this is of major interest in the illustrated Bibles—she sees the sinful ways of the world and, not the least, the vices of the clergy. Amorous couples always appear in the perilous proximity of devils who are ready to drag them off.[22] Ecclesia sees this and warns, instructs, grieves.

In the great questions of life and death, doctrine and judgment, Synagoga gives a preliminary but unsatisfactory answer, just as the foolish virgins had given the wrong answer. Synagoga is perplexed and helpless, while demons lead her protégés off to hell. She must die and will die over and over until the right answer is found or can be revealed. Just as there are stages of revelation, so there are stages of awareness, and Synagoga is the symbol of this. She is transitory, whereas Ecclesia, as an idea and type, stands outside of time in ideal contemporaneousness with all events in human history.

The timeless, mystical Ecclesia grew out of personified wisdom in the Proverbs of Solomon. Fostered by biblical typology she lived on through the centuries of the Middle Ages and finally was portrayed in the personal atmosphere of the miniaturists, far from the official art of the church. As an allegory of God's timelessness, the *werdelos* (literally, undeveloping) divinity, as later mystics were to say, she could establish an undogmatic relationship with her traditional opponent, Synagoga—indeed, could assimilate her as a stage of spiritual development.

The Bamberg and Strasbourg figures of Ecclesia and Synagoga are in the conciliatory spirit of this view, which continued in contemporary and later miniatures. To be sure, Synagoga was still associated with the Old Testament and by implication with medieval Jewry, but the impression prevailed that her blindness is the fate of *all* mortals and that she, still more nature than spirit, represented only a first stage of awareness. In the destiny of the individual, as in that of entire peoples, this stage must be surmounted again and again by the pure and eternal spirit, which stands above all nature. In the hidden paths of thought of the mystics this conciliatory view slowly became imageless and ineffable. "Everything one can apprehend about God is not God" (Meister Eckhart).

IV

At the same time there arose from this constantly ramifying symbolism a new figure: Mary the Queen of Heaven, *mater et sponsa Christi.* The growing worship of the Virgin Mary transferred the emblems of Ecclesia, the mantle and crown, to the new Queen of Heaven; the mysticism of the *Ecclesia universalis* was continued in the mysticism surrounding the figure of the Holy Virgin. Every stage of revelation and grace, the entire history of salvation, Christian and pre-Christian, was contained in her. The Virgin Mary became the all-encompassing symbol of Christian belief, the successor to the inheritance of Ecclesia.

The generation of Suger, the *Ludus* poet, and Bernard of Clairvaux, which had overcome the religious conflict, was creative here as well. The speculative means were supplied by the typological relationships. Ivo of Chartres transferred Christ's relationship with Ecclesia to that with His mother; Honorius of Autun spoke frequently of the conjugal relationship of Christ and Mary. In the typological sense Christ became the "second Adam" and Mary the "second Eve." Just as the tempter laid a snare with Eve, so the mercy of God creates a refuge in Mary. In a strict typological sense, fulfilling and heightening what has preceded, the name *Eva* became a figuration of the *Ave* Maria:

> Taking the AVE
> From Gabriel's lips
> Place us in the state of peace
> By transforming the name of EVA.[23]

Since Eva was also the type of Ecclesia, the equating of Ecclesia with Mary occurred here as it did in Bernard's sermons: he spoke of Eve as the *ministra seductionis* and of Mary as the *ministra reductionis*. The century experienced an increasing adoration of Mary in religious speculation, sermons, and songs. This worship of Mary was stimulated by the knightly code of love that was developing at the time. Heavenly love ennobles the earthly, and earthly love becomes a forerunner of the love of God.

The worship of Mary found expression in monumental statuary in the great cathedrals, dedicated to "Our Lady," of the twelfth and thirteenth centuries. The ornamental statuary on the façades culminates here in the coronation of Mary high above the prophets, apostles, Ecclesia, and Synagoga. As *vierge dorée*, Mary stands at the center pillar of the portals. It was Dante again who formulated the new experience of Mary-worship. His prayer to Mary to be admitted to the presence of God he attributed to St. Bernard, the creator of the cult of Mary:

> Maiden and Mother, daughter of thine own Son,
> Beyond all creatures lowly and lifted high,
> Of the Eternal Design the corner-stone!

Thou art she who did man's substance glorify
So that its own Maker did not eschew
Even to be made of its mortality [*Paradiso* 33].[24]

Thus for a long period of time two groups of symbols were side by side: the older pair of Ecclesia and Synagoga, and Mary the Queen of Heaven. Both groups were representatives of the same great idea, but differed in nature and in depth of religious effect. The principal differences lay in the fact that Ecclesia and Synagoga were allegorical figures that originated in scriptural passages and were transformed into living characters only by means of great art; Mary's development, on the other hand, went far beyond the often forced typology. Another difference was the complicated thought system of *Concordia* connected with the figures of Ecclesia and Synagoga. The equilibrium of this thought system was extremely delicate, always endangered by latent hostility, and maintained only by eschatological certainty.

Mary, on the other hand, was the human vessel of divine will, and as virgin, mother, and bride of Christ was free from all perils. Every contradiction was resolved in her. In addition, she was more than just a figure of eschatological proportions: she was the intercessor who was called upon for help; she was not doctrine, but love. Here the piety of the people could find greater satisfaction; the world of the woman as maiden, bride, and mother had been built into the symbolic structure of religion.

In thee is pity, in thee is tenderness,
In thee magnificence, in thee the sum
Of all that in creation most can bless [*Paradiso* 33].

The monuments of art confirm this simultaneous existence of Ecclesia and Mary, their secret rivalry, indeed, the interchangeability of both figures, which became almost identical.[25]

On the tympanum above the Golden Portal in Freiberg (ca. 1225), God crowns Mary with the same gesture of lofty simplicity as in the crowning of Ecclesia in the window of St. Denis. In miniatures of the apocalypse,[26] which date from the same period and are related to Codex Latinus 11560 in Paris, the heavenly pair of Christ and Ecclesia appear, the latter "adorned like a bride for her bridegroom" (Fig. 51). The manner of representation is that of a crowning of Mary with the exception of the chalice in the middle of the picture, which had not yet been replaced by the globe of the world that is found in scenes of the coronation of the Virgin (and once an emblem of Ecclesia).

In the great Codex Latinus 11560, which originated during and after the generation of the Bamberg and Strasbourg masters, Ecclesia, teimeless as on the day of creation, is a witness to the birth of Christ (Fig. 53). She stands under the curtain, which is being drawn far back and is an allusion to the blindfold of Synagoga: an abbreviated form for the world of associations. This design was repeated in the later Codex Fr. 167.

This combination of motifs in the decisive meeting of Ecclesia and Mary at the birth of the Christ Child appeared again about 1410 in the illuminated manuscript begun by Paul of Limburg and his brothers for Duke Philipp of Burgundy (Fig. 54).[27] This was one of the last significant portrayals of Ecclesia: the tablets of Moses in her hand show her to be the custodian of the Old Testament treasure as well; as the substitute for Synagoga she is a timeless witness of the word that became incarnate in her.

This union of the Old Testament and Ecclesia also elucidates the meaning of the "Candelabra Angel" on the tympanum above the narthex in Freiburg. The Freiburg Cathedral is a church of Mary, and Ecclesia and Synagoga are only members of the procession in the narthex and opponents in the tournament in the Tucher window. The adoration of Mary determines the nature of the decorative statuary in the cathedral. The Madonna and Child stand at the center pillar of the portal, and among the reliefs on the tympanum the most space is devoted to the birth of Christ. In the axis of the composition, a regal woman with crown and candelabra stands at the head of the crib (Fig. 55)—certainly not an angel, but rather Ecclesia, holding a candelabra instead of a chalice, and witnessing the birth of Christ.

Finally, a trace of the *Ecclesia universalis* can still be found in the Isenheim Altar by Matthias Grünewald (Fig. 56) where the figure merges with that of Mary. In the divine splendor and radiance of her halo and with a flaming crown on her head she appears as the "Mary before the time," as she is known among the people. Before her stands a glass vessel, the symbol of the virgin birth. She is worshipping the Child, who is held out toward her by the Mary of the Nativity. The timelessness of Ecclesia, who was present even at the creation, the "little spark" of Meister Eckhart, leads into this "Mary before the time" who, in the garb of the Mary of the Annunciation becomes a witness of Christ's birth, just like Ecclesia in the older miniatures. In her timelessness she extends into the future: in her visionary prayer she already anticipates Christ's resurrection.

At this point, the history of Ecclesia in church art essentially came to an end, though it was at times re-evoked. On the ceiling of the Sistine Chapel, Eve, the type of Ecclesia, still uncreated yet present, peers forth from the great fold of God's mantle, "still unfettered by fate, an undesecrated divine idea . . ." (C. F. Meyer). She is yearning for Adam, the type of Christ, who is just being created, and for the *unio mystica* (Fig. 57). And again later, in Bach's Cantata 140, Ecclesia celebrated her last, unforgettable return.

Chapter 12

The End of the Great Symbol

Everything that exists is from God, and even in evil
and in wicked men his order prevails;
but I must confess that I am perplexed by the contradiction
between the fact that no one is without God
and that God is nevertheless not with everyone.
—ST. AUGUSTINE,
De ordine II, 20

I

In the twelfth and thirteenth centuries the polemical antinomy between Ecclesia and Synagoga merged into an eschatologically determined synthesis; in the following period, however, it again came to life, as was shown by the connection of this theme with that of the wise and foolish virgins. In the passion plays, which experienced a rapid development in the growing cities from the middle of the thirteenth century on, irreconcilability, a legacy from the prophet play, became a central theme.

The passion plays were organized and presented on a regular basis by church groups and guilds in the course of the church year. The settings for these productions were marketplaces and main streets. Participating organizations vied with one another in elaborateness of presentation to increase the appeal of these popular festivals. The passion plays show to what a great extent the liturgical drama underlying them could bc secularized and the religious core consumed by low humor, spite, and sensationalism. At the same time, basically insignificant scenes were exploited for their tendentious effect: for example, Joseph's being troubled by the yet unborn child of the Holy Ghost; the boasting, drunken mercenaries at the foot of the cross who cast lots for the Savior's clothes; and the domestic worries of the merchant who sells the ointments to Mary Magdalene. Often the Jews were the focus of public ridicule in these dramas. The influence of the passion plays was considerable and it seems that a number of conceptions in popular arts and crafts were taken over from the plays. What is of interest to us are the roles that Ecclesia and Synagoga had to assume in the passion plays.[1] Here the dispute between the two women, which we must assume had been developing in pageants and presentations long before the monumental statuary, finally appeared in literary form.

The so-called Frankfurt Stage Directions [2] contains directions and cues, partially in Latin, relative to the dispute of the two women. Despite the incompleteness of the text it becomes clear that a principal concern of the Frankfurt drama was the conversion of Jews who, after the horrors of the Black Death, were again the victims of persecution and proselytism.

The drama, like the *Christmas Play of Benediktbeuren*, commences with the prophet play, but the tone and comedy are coarser and the prophecies interrupted by heckling from the Jews on stage. They deride David and Solomon for their amorous adventures. St. Augustine puts an end to the controversy: to make clear to doubters the invalidity of their objections, the passion is presented, ending with the ascension of Christ.

The disputation does not come until later, in an epilogue. Here the theme of the prophet play is again taken up, thus forming a framework for the entire production.

Ecclesia: *Domine, da rectum. . . .*
[O Father Jesus Christ, give us what is just]

Synagoga: *Nos alium dominum nescimus. . . .*
[We know no other Lord]

Ecclesia then implores the crowd of Jews led by Synagoga to renounce their false belief. "Eight or ten" Jews accept baptism, which completely breaks the heart of proud Synagoga.

Haec videns Synagoga tristi animo cantat:
[When Synagoga sees this she exclaims dejectedly:]

Synagoga: *Israel popule carissime. . . .*
[Israel, people dearest to me]

Hic Synagoga cadit pallium de humeris et corona de capite:
[The mantle falls from her shoulders, and the crown from her head:]

Quo facto Ecclesia laetabundo animo cantat.
[Jubilantly Ecclesia proclaims her victory.]

Together, all exclaim, "Christ is arisen!"

The Frankfurt Stage Directions served as a model for several passion plays, among which the Ahlsfeld passion play of 1501 is the best known.[3] In this version Synagoga is replaced by a man, the Synagogus,[4] who remains on stage for the entire duration of the passion play and is the instigator of all the evil committed by the Jews. He punctuates the miracles and sayings of Jesus with spiteful remarks; he demands the death sentence from Caiaphas and Pontius Pilate for the alleged impostor; he is the first to cry "crucify him!"; and he observes the sufferings of the Savior with diabolic pleasure. The disputation between him and Ecclesia is the longest single episode in the entire drama, full of crudities, mutual insults, and vulgar allusions. Toward the end of the long argument Ecclesia says:

"Thus I must end this matter
And blind you evil Jews
So that you and all your children
Are blind despite your healthy vision . . .
And send you all at once
Into the deep abyss of hell. . . ."

The passion play of Donaueschingen (late fifteenth century) is the only German text in which Ecclesia and Synagoga are described outwardly. It states: "Enter Christiana the Queen, dressed in beautiful garments and looking like a Christian, holding a little red banner with a golden cross . . . Judea, another queen, is dressed like a Jewess and has a banner in her hand, which is yellow with a black idol. . . ."[5]

As in the early ivories, the disputation is here again related to the crucifixion. Ecclesia warns that the Jews will have to suffer bitter vengeance for the death of Christ. After the resurrection the disputation continues; without giving Synagoga any chance to reply, Ecclesia states, "As a sign that you are all blind and have a false belief I blindfold your eyes and break your flagstaff in two. . . ."

In these two passion plays of Ahlsfeld and Donaueschingen the eschatological symbol is completely reversed. The church itself binds the eyes of the Jews as punishment for the death of Christ and for the obstinacy with which they resist conversion. The veil of blindness and death is irrevocable, like the arrow that the devil shoots into Synagoga's eye in the passion window in Chartres (Fig. 20). Vulgar exhibition has perverted the original conflict and filled it with plain hatred.

One factor contributing indirectly to this decline of the theme in the passion plays may have been the constant memories of the excesses of the pogroms. The distorted characterizations betray, perhaps, a latent endeavor to justify those excesses by allowing the grotesque Jews in the drama to commit senseless acts of cruelty against the Savior, as in the Ahlsfeld passion play. The baneful identification of medieval Jewry with the "murderers of Christ," which began at the time of the crusades and would inevitably destroy the eschatological idea, reaches its high point of vulgarity. In the last scene of an English play, where the Jews and other sinners are condemned to the eternal torments of hell, even God's tribunal on judgment day is subject to this verdict:

In helle to dwelle with-outen ende;
There ye shall nevere but sorowe see
And sitte be Satanas the fende.[6]

The triumph of the mob over *Concordia* and the unleashing of demonic powers through misused symbolism can be seen in the following two quotations:

In the dramas of the late medieval period the Jews are treated with ridicule and contempt; in the antichrist drama their joy over the long-awaited Messiah who would supposedly destroy Christianity is described in grotesque detail. . . . In the Tegernsee *Ludus de Anti-*

christo nothing of this sort had been expressed, and in the antichrist dramas of the fourteenth century the dreadful extent that hatred of the Jews had reached even at that early time was barely perceptible. The situation was clearly different when, in 1469, the antichrist drama was presented in Frankfurt; now the officials felt obliged to take special measures for the protection of the Jewish quarter during the performance.[7]

> The real low point for our symbols [Ecclesia and Synagoga] in church art coincides precisely in time with the greatest degradation of the Jewish people. All types of literary works that are considered here—the hymns, clerical dramas, and the Shrovetide plays—exude the same hatred and contempt as the contemporary pictures, the numerous woodcuts in Hartmann Schedel's *World Chronicle*, or the innumerable lampoons of the Jews, which found a convenient means of dissemination in the popular techniques of woodcarving and copper engraving that were then being developed.[8]

The symbol, robbed of its original idea, had become a means of expressing anger at medieval Jewry. Other documents also attest to the fact that the Jewish quarters had to be sealed off when passion plays were being presented. There was a danger that the damnation of the Jews, which was expressed and protrayed in full public view, would be translated into action. The power of dramatic illusion and the magic of the word, which were so clearly perceived by Gerhoh von Reichersberg (Chapter 8)—who for this reason rejected the drama on principle—here display their demagogic impact. Whatever historical and social factors may be involved in anti-Semitism, the conflict became virtually insoluble at that time because the Jews' natural right to call upon the same God as the Christians had been denied them and their freedom of belief curtailed.

II

The passion plays reduced Ecclesia and Synagoga to figures in the realm of popular entertainment; the intrinsic distance from *Concordia*, the Christian theology that had taken shape in monumental statuary, could hardly have been greater. Religious art lost interest in the two female figures, one of which was already in the process of transformation into Mary the Queen of Heaven and Mother of God, while the other is dragged into the streets by anti-Semitism and banished to the underworld of demonic beings.[9]

The last dignified, large-scale representation of Synagoga is in a painting by Conrad Witz dating from about 1430 (Fig. 58). The panel was intended for an altar with several scenes from the Old and New Testaments in a traditional arrangement. Synagoga appears once more in monumental proportions as a young woman who must withdraw from the scene. Her downcast eyes make the blindfold almost superfluous—it is only a delicate, transparent veil. She is not cast out by some external force but follows tragic necessity. The angle of the open door toward which she must go underlines with magical force the break in the lance. The door itself leads away from life. From then on the dogmatic and didactic allegory prevailed in art, above all in the portrayal of the "Living Cross." [10]

In this portrayal an uncanny life is bestowed on the cross itself. The beams are provided with a crown and sword held by arms that grow out of the cross and that take an active part in the *disputatio* or the tournament between the two queens. This manner of representation derived from scholarly theological allegory that was given a popular interpretation. In one instance Synagoga rides on her sacrificial animal, the goat; in another, she is astride a stumbling donkey whose hocks have been cut. In other cases she carries the head of a donkey. Rats lap up the blood. Ecclesia rides her tetramorph or kneels at the foot of the cross, while opposite her a female idol collapses beneath the sword. Sometimes Ecclesia's place is taken by a priest or even by the pope celebrating the mass. In a mural in Bruneck, Tyrol (ca. 1526), Mary stands beside the kneeling Ecclesia while Synagoga on her bleeding donkey receives the deathblow. Behind them stand Eve and an allegory of death.

As an example of the others, we may take the initial *A* in the Codex Monacensis 23041 (Fig. 59), which originated in the last decade of the fifteenth century. An elaborate composition on a gold background shows the crucified Lord with God the Father and six angels, and beneath them the tournament of the two queens. A hand from one of the arms growing out of the cross thrusts a sword into Synagoga's head. In the foreground

Christ, with the banner of victory, descends into hell, where the patriarchs are awaiting him. Behind them, in the center field and to the right, one sees Eve with the serpent, as she plucks the apple; opposite her stands Ecclesia, representing the church, with a crown and staff of the cross, spreading the folds of her mantle over her protégés. Again we find the symbolic division of the picture into a side of life and a side of death, as first seen in the Uta evangelistary (ca. 1050). To the left of the cross, hell, the fall of man, and Synagoga are depicted; on Christ's right we find Ecclesia on her tetramorph and the figure with the protective mantle. This is an example of the equating of Ecclesia with Mary. The so-called Madonna in the Protective Mantle became a frequent and popular motif at just that time, near the end of the fifteenth century.[11]

There is only one example of a "Living Cross" by a well-known artist. Benvenuto Tisi, known as Garofalo and a pupil of Raphael, painted such a work in Ferrara in 1532.[12] The last example of a "Living Cross" is found as a woodcut in a collection of curios in the *Lectiones memorabiles et reconditae*, printed in 1600. It is also the last portrayal of the two women. After a history of eight centuries in European art, they came to an undignified and obscure end, while the social conditions that they witnessed transformed the religious motif into a "race question."

III

Yet other allegories originated in the area of Spanish and Flemish culture, where the Catholic church, with the help of the state, successfully combated the popular Reformation movement. An example is the great "Christ Giving the Blessing" in the Prado, which for a long time was considered to be a work of Jan van Eyck and only recently has been attributed to the Spaniard Fernando Gallego. Here, too, Ecclesia and Synagoga were derived from the conception in the miniatures. The large panels depicting "The Fountain of Life or the Triumph of the Church over the Synagogue," which have been preserved in several copies,[13] likewise originated among the Spanish pupils of Van Eyck. The work was patterned after Van Eyck's altarpiece in Ghent and is identical to it in many details. In the foreground a *disputatio* is depicted: on the left, dignitaries of the church and state reverently worship the Eucharist, which is dispensed by the "Fountain of Life." Opposite them, the Jews reject the Sacrament of Holy Communion in a highly dramatic scene. Ecclesia and Synagoga themselves no longer appear in this dispute; the role of Synagoga has been taken over by medieval Jews who refuse to accept conversion. In keeping with this observation is the assumption that this portrayal celebrates a miracle that is said to have taken place in Segovia following the desecration of the host by the Jews.

Finally, a woodcut from the workshop of Hans Burgkmair should be mentioned. It was used as the frontispiece of a humanist drama, a Latin *disputatio*, published by Johannes Stamler in Augsburg in 1508.[14] In this *disputatio* a rabbi and a Mohammedan confront the doctors of theology. The learned rabbi supports the Mohammedan by pointing to the yet unfulfilled promises of Christ and the failures of the church. But both are won over in the end and ask to be baptized. The woodcut (Fig. 60) shows the *Sancta Mater Ecclesia* on her throne, flanked by the pope and the emperor, to whom she gives keys and a sword. Four women with broken flagstaffs—Saracena, Sinagoga, Gentilitas, and Tartarica—sit humbly around the throne as subjects of the church and the empire, while in the foreground the learned Doctor Oliverius leads the religious discussion. Interestingly, the pointed hat of the Jews is found on the banner of Saracena, while on Sinagoga's banner the name Machometus appears. One could regard this interchanging of the banners simply as an error on the part of the woodcarver who was unfamiliar with the previous history of his allegories. More likely, however, is the assumption that the Jews were thereby being accused of collusion with the Turks, the enemies of the nation; both were enemies of Christianity. Thus, to the many accusations heaped upon the Jews in the late Middle Ages, that of treason and conspiracy with the Turks was added.

Chapter 13

Literary Evidence of *Concordia*

Art is the surest means of withdrawing from the world, and at the same time there is no surer way of involving oneself with the world than through art.

—GOETHE

The historical conflict is expressed in a number of literary monuments that lie outside the theme of Ecclesia and Synagoga. Here, as in other works of the highest quality, artistic mastery was combined with the spirit of *Concordia.* We take as examples the *Divine Comedy* of Dante, the *Decameron* of Boccaccio and the *Easter Play of Redentin.*

In the *Inferno* Dante staged a dress rehearsal of the last judgment and appointed himself temporary judge, but his verdict did not populate the underworld with Jews. Numerous contemporary portrayals of hell show how unique this attitude was. To be sure, Judas suffers eternal torment in the lowest orbit of hell; however, he does so not as a Jew, but as the betrayer of the Lord. He finds himself there in the company of Brutus and Cassius, who, according to the medieval view, betrayed the temporal order (*Inferno* 34). Judas is punished as an individual; as far as the Jews are concerned, the destruction of Jerusalem by the Romans was punishment enough (*Paradiso* 6). After all, it was neither Herod nor Caiaphas who pronounced the death sentence, but the Roman Pontius Pilate.

With ever increasing scrupulousness, Dante becomes lost in the apparent contradiction between historical and religious guilt, until Beatrice shows him the way out of this quandary (*Paradiso* 7). In the *Divine Comedy* there is not the remotest allusion to even one of the many slogans expressing the anti-Semitism so common in Dante's time. The *Paradiso* celebrates *Concordia* in constantly new allegories and symbols, among which the "Heavenly Rose" is the most striking (*Paradiso* 32). What Dante claimed as the highest calling and responsibility of the poet—"to lead mankind back to the right path"—is discharged in this manner.

The example given by Boccaccio is even more striking, in view of the polemical intensification that the theme experienced in his time in connection with the Black Death. The frame tale of the *Decameron* gives a vivid description of life in the cities that had been ravaged by the plague. This was a convenient opportunity to repeat the crude accusation that Jews had poisoned the wells. But Boccaccio did not give even a hint of this. An even greater temptation for him lay in his often trenchant satirical genius, but he did not indulge his wit at the expense of the Jews. The second story of the first day tells how the Jew Abraham converts to the Christian faith despite the depravity of the priests that he has witnessed at the papal court in Rome. The focus of attention is first of all the Jew, then his Christian friend, and then Christianity as a doctrine, all being praised in turn. The only reproach is reserved for the morals of the clergy. The tale is an ingenious paraphrase of an old proverbial expression (which Boccaccio made use of in the text) to the effect that Christian doctrine must really be inspired by the Holy Ghost, since it "continues to grow and increase in glory and majesty" despite the zeal and cunning employed by the clergy in its attempts "to destroy it and drive it from the face of the earth."

This old adage had a long previous history going back to heretical literature and advanced the claim that educated laymen in their piety and wisdom stand closer to the fountainhead of religion than its official representatives.

The third story of the first day is that of the three rings, which the Jew Melchisedeck tells to Sultan Saladin. Although the deep-seated skepticism of orthodoxy, which was then in vogue among the educated laity, is given expression here, the equality of the three monotheistic religions is also proclaimed: they all possess equal rank and justification, as well as truth and error. This story also has its forerunners; it can be traced back to enlightened and heretical groups at the court of the Hohenstaufen King Frederick II of Sicily. It was thus already one hundred years old when Boccaccio gave it lasting form in his *Decameron.* Four hundred years later the tale was again taken up by Gotthold Ephraim Lessing, who placed it at the focal point of his drama *Nathan the Wise.*

Among the passion plays and mystery plays originating in the late Middle Ages, the *Easter Play of Redentin* [1] stands out for its remarkable unity of time and action as well as for its dramatic values. It was written in the Low German dialect by a Cistercian monk, Peter Kalt, in 1464. The comical element is, of course, not missing but was kept within bounds and not allowed to detract from the basic spirit.

The widespread, popular allusions to the Jews were, it would seem, scrupulously avoided. Pontius Pilate appears as a German feudal prince presiding over his court of justice. His hirelings are braggarts and knightly highwaymen, but not Jews; their names consist of a mixture of Hebraic elements and German titles of nobility. The lines "I thrust the spear in his heart / and he suffered the pain of death" (verses 411–12) are spoken by Satan and not, as in many other plays, by Jews. The play contains a stern warning to all Christians not to embrace the Jewish faith, but there is no demand that the Jews accept baptism.

In the second part it is stated that hell must be repopulated after Christ has redeemed the patriarchs and prophets of the Old Covenant who had been there. Yet, there is never any suggestion that Jews primarily might be these children of the devil. On the contrary, it is the "good" citizens who are brought together in hell, where each must atone for the specific sins of his social class.

Medieval anti-Semitism, which makes itself so painfully evident in most plays of this sort, is here limited to lighthearted jesting. Whereas in a Frankfurt drama the Jews are given names of local Jewish families or, in other dramas, dance around speaking a gibberish supposedly sounding like Yiddish, here they appear in a dignified light, even when they pay the mercenaries and must support the latter's claims to be re-engaged by Pontius Pilate.

Chapter 14

The Humanistic-Protestant Sequel

Whatsoever in a thousand books may come to you
as truth or fiction is but a Tower of Babel
unless by love united.
—GOETHE

I

The Reformation did not have a salutary influence on the old problem of the relationship between Christians and Jews. To be sure, the Old Testament retained its traditional rank as the preliminary stage to the New Testament, but this association did not give rise to any constructive communal forces. Christian humanism, which helped pave the way for the Reformation and had generated the hopeful beginnings of a reconciliation between Jews and Christians, was really not able to bring it about in the long run.

Johann Reuchlin published the first Hebrew grammar in 1506, making possible the study of Hebrew on a scholarly basis. He admired the primeval wisdom of man in Jewish literature and believed he had discovered close relationships between Jewish mysticism as set forth in the cabala and the truths of Christian faith.[1] The essence of Christianity was for him not that which separates church and synagogue but that which is common to both: belief in God. The religious conflict again stood under the judgment of God and a genuine dialogue whose outcome was not dogmatically predetermined would have been possible. The *Concordia* of the Carolingian Renaissance (cf. Chapter 5) seemed to be repeating itself in a situation that was both religiously and culturally similar. Reuchlin also anticipated some of the ideas of Jakob Böhme, Pietism, and the universal theism of the eighteenth century. Hardly any of these possibilities contained in Christian humanism were carried over into the Reformation in the sixteenth century.

At first Luther saw in the Judaism of his time only the typical fate of man without God: intellectual vanity that believes it can do without God's mercy and self-righteousness that can be heightened to the point of godlessness. Thus, the synagogue was, to Luther, at first merely a stage of spiritual development that had to be overcome, as in the tradition of *Ecclesia universalis*. Luther always sought to maintain the oneness of all human guilt, Jewish as well as Christian, but he believed he saw with particular clarity the godless, self-righteous side of human nature in the case of the synagogue. His position was, therefore, hardly different from that of the medieval church in its dialogue with the Jews. He did not share Reuchlin's desire for a more complete understanding of Jewish mysticism, but saw in it principally a missionary task for his church.

Later, in the consolidation of the Protestant church, Luther encountered the active countermission of the synagogue. Here, too, a phenomenon of the Carolingian Renaissance reappeared. The Jews experienced their own far-reaching religious movement and in so doing often came in contact with sects on the fringes of protestantism. Luther, when older, took a vigorous stand both against the sects and against the attempts by the Jews to interpret and turn to their own advantage the general crisis of Christianity. He believed it his duty to warn Christians of the Jewish countermission, and he did it in such a way that the medieval disputation also occurred in a number of his writings. Profound theological insights were overshadowed by the fear that Christians might make the mistake of yielding and thus fall victim to the judgment that God had pronounced on the Jews. In this struggle Luther indulged in abusive words, which conveyed the bitter polemics of medieval anti-Semitism, to his Protestant readers—to be sure, not without encountering opposition.[2]

II

In addition to the events just described, which grew out of the antinomy between religion and society, there were other factors that brought to an end the history of the two biblical queens. Even the earliest forerunners of humanism had discovered in the intellectual world of antiquity another line of descent for Christian doctrine, in addition to the one that was contained in the Old Testament and symbolically represented by Synagoga.

From early times Christianity was indebted to Neoplatonism, the source of Christian mysticism. St. Thomas Aquinas propounded the revolutionary thesis that Aristotelian philosophy also was compatible with church doctrine. In the very next generation the world of antiquity made broad advances into medieval culture. Dante implored the muses while calling Christ the highest Jupiter. "Gods, heroes, fabulous creatures of antiquity, old and new ideated deities pervade his wonderful three-fold realm and joyfully and willingly serve the Christian God" (E. Peterich).

Dante was convinced that human morality had the power to bring man to the portal of Paradise. Vergil had for a long time been associated with the prophets of Christ; now he was called upon to lead the stumbling Dante through hell to the "Mountain of Purgatory." The human spirit, represented in exemplary fashion by Vergil, is able to guide man to the threshhold of bliss; in order to cross over it, Vergil was lacking only baptism. Dante respected this Christian principle. With muted yet never suppressed emotion, he let Vergil suspect and indicate that Limbo[3] cannot really be the abode of the pure and perfected spirits of classical times.

We have here a religious evaluation of antiquity to which Dante made his prophetic contribution in the figure of Vergil; an evaluation that, in the centuries to follow, was recurrently discovered, interpreted, and accepted. Humanism ushered in a new cultural awareness that was also prepared, in religious matters, to look beyond the bounds of church doctrine and to project into the entire human spectrum—the antique and contemporary, Old Testament and Christian—a new, lofty vision of man. This vision was in many respects similar to the antique view and enriched the traditional Christian image of man. Beneath this so greatly expanded firmament, purely biblical allegories lost their significance. Ecclesia had already been transformed into the Queen of Heaven; and Synagoga, who as an artistic concept lived on only because of the biblical allegory, would have been no match for the splendor and newly discovered humanity of the female characters of antiquity, even if she had been spared the scorn of medieval anti-Semitism.

The transformation in meaning of medieval allegories, which was inevitable in the humanistic era, can be shown with particular clarity in the case of the wise and foolish maidens. This motif had been transformed from an eschatological parable into a lesson on virtue dealing with sexual chastity and unchastity and appeared repeatedly in the processions of the maidens on cathedral portals, frequently in the entourage of Ecclesia and Synagoga. In the Renaissance this moral lesson was to a large extent forgotten; the motif of the maidens was felt to be antiquated and had to be reinterpreted.

In woodcuts by Niklaus Manuel Deutsch we see the lansquenets' camp prostitutes in whose hands the cruse of oil looks like an outmoded implement that is scornfully cast aside (Figs. 61 and 62). In a contemporary copper engraving by Urs Graf, the foolish virgin removes her last article of clothing while contemptuously casting the oil lamp aside. From out of the medieval costume emerges *Venus naturalis*, the goddess of antiquity, who had always made sport with the foolish virgins and now can openly tread underfoot the globe of the earth (Fig. 63).

III

The pagan sibyls had previously been elevated to positions as sisters of the prophets; the ideas of the classical pre-Christian world were now brought together with biblical doctrine, and classical antiquity was accepted as the second line of descent of Christianity. The Renaissance took possession of the newly discovered territory and repeatedly gave new form and meaning to the humanistic allegories, while the purely Christian themes—the birth of Christ, the holy family, the flight into Egypt, the last supper, Gethsemane, and the crucifixion—could now appear in a more human light, free from allegorical trappings.

The fresh-flowing source of the pre-Christian, pagan outlook on life in close association with church tradition inspired Raphael, at the age of only twenty-five, to paint the frescoes for the Stanza della Segnatura. In the "Disputà" (Triumph of Religion) he once more erected the entire cosmos of medieval faith extending from God the Father and Christ to the monstrance. The mystery of the Lord's supper is surrounded by witnesses to the Old and New Covenants—the prophets, apostles, and saints. The old dualism of Ecclesia and Synagoga disappeared in the hierarchy of faith. On the opposite wall Raphael painted the "School of Athens," that second line of ancestors that had just been legitimized and in which the struggle of pre-Christian times for ultimate truth was made visible in illustrious personages: Plato, Aristotle, Socrates, Heraclitus, Pythagoras—even Averroës, Zoroaster, and numerous others appear. Dante's Limbo is raised up out of the twilight of *Inferno*, where it had been surrounded by darkness, into the lustrous proximity of salvation.

In the third fresco, the "Parnassus," these august groups are joined by the poets of antiquity. Dante, who more than any other person was responsible for the interpretation of this pagan lineage of Christendom, is of course also present. The claim of redemption for antiquity, which he expressed quietly and hesitantly, had become a sweeping manifesto that could no longer be ignored: the program and vital essence of the Renaissance.

The new *Concordia* that was achieved in the three frescoes goes far beyond the dualism of the Old and New Covenants. With a fervent single-mindedness it traced all the manifestations of human accomplishment theretofore known, and drew its inspiration from them.

At the same time that Raphael created his frescoes in the Stanza della Segnatura, Michelangelo was painting the sibyls and prophets in the Sistine Chapel. Here, too, the new alliance of Christianity with antiquity is revealed, to be sure, not as a multi-tiered religious cosmos as in Raphael's painting but in the older tradition: Michelangelo limited himself to the one dimension of the history of salvation, but he did it with the force of a personal engagement.

IV

Bach's Cantata No. 140 was written for the twenty-seventh Sunday after Trinity and celebrated the biblical passage prescribed for that day, the parable of the wise and foolish virgins. As a basis and framework, Bach chose the hymn "Wachet auf, ruft uns die Stimme" (Awake, the voice is calling us) by Philipp Nicolai (1599), who had transferred this parable to the Protestant hymnbook, thus imparting to Bach's contemporaries —above all, to the Pietists—both the mystical experience of Christian love and the mystic wedding.[4] Bach went beyond this first theme, however, interweaving it with the figures of the Song of Solomon: Zion, the wise virgin of the first theme is also the beloved in whose praise the Song of Solomon was conceived. By virtue of the affinity of the two themes, which Bach sensed and which inspired him, the love lyric of the Old Testament combines with the mystic wedding that is anticipated in the parable of the virgins. Both themes utilize the experience of human love as a bridge to the transcendental and the divine.

With both themes Bach touched upon essential matters in the medieval development of Ecclesia and Synagoga; for the virgins belong to the entourage of the two biblical queens (see Chapter 10), and the beloved celebrated in the Song of Solomon is an Old Testament type of Ecclesia (Chapter 3). This fact justifies our examining the two themes in the cantata, even though there is no suggestion in Bach's composition of the phases of development of Ecclesia and Synagoga. The historical dualism of the two queens has been assimilated in the higher unity of universal belief in God.

Despite the intended focus on daily life, the parable of the virgins never lost its original context and was handed down to Bach's time in this dual role. The awareness that this is not only the wedding day but also the day of judgment lives on in a pietistic "Wedding Song":

God comes to punish the world,
To wreak his fury and vengeance
On all who are not wakeful
And who worship the beast's image
Together with the dragon.[5]

Along with the wise virgins of this "Wedding Song" who prepare to receive the bridegroom—their judge—the image is re-evoked of the foolish virgins who thoughtlessly persist in their disbelief and who worship "the beast's image." Characteristically, Bach does not include this legal aspect in his cantata; it is also missing in Nicolai's hymn. Bach's virgins are pure expectation, readiness, and faith. They are timeless and stand outside the historical conflict of the two queens.

Bach's second theme, the Song of Songs, as the type of Ecclesia and symbol of the *unio mystica*, is also a biblical idea. The mystic wedding is not only the union of Ecclesia with Christ in the image of the Song of Songs but signifies, above all, the ever-recurring wedding of the soul to God. The soul is the bride; God—that is, Christ—is the bridegroom. "This love that brings the soul to the divine word and makes the word so familiar that the soul ventures to express its desires . . . is this not the bond of a sacred marriage? A sweet communion, but a brief moment and a rare experience."[6]

This symbolic bridge from the physical to the spiritual, from the earthly to the eternal, had been generally accepted by Christians since the time of Bernard, was given form by Dante, and still conveyed to Pietism a vivid immediacy. The intimacy of the antiphony in Bach's cantata draws strength from this mystical source, and its melodies give the biblical text an inimitable interpretation. The mutual proximity of human and divine love is expressed repeatedly in sublime allusions. The musical motifs of yearning and devotion intensify in the antiphony of the lovers, finally coming together in the words "Nothing shall divide love," whereupon the magnificent "Gloria" in the last strophe of the choral commences.

Bach placed the text of the Song of Songs and the antiphony in the broad intervals of the three choral strophes.

They produce an effect simliar to that of highly artistic choir-screens between columns of a cathedral. The objective system of *Ecclesia triumphans*, which is founded on these three columns and culminates in the "Gloria" as in an arched vault, is imbued here with a highly personal experience of love and is inwardly confirmed. The joyous, festive march of the wedding procession in the introduction is continued in the first choral strophe, is heard again in the recitative of the watchman, and remains perceptible—at times distant, then closer—until the opening of the wedding hall. Characteristic is the role of the oboe, the ancient instrument of pastoral love: as early as the second section this instrument rises both sensuously and devoutly above the accompanying melodies and maintains the lead in the dialogue of love, gladsome in its inherent union of nature and spirit.

In Bach's cantata "Wachet auf," beauty as a religious concept is experienced in just as imposing a manner as in the Bamberg and Strasbourg sisters and in the work of Dante and Michelangelo. The equating of *amor dei*, *ordo*, and *pulchritudo*, which Dante had set up (see Chapter 10), is also valid for Bach's cantata and found renewed confirmation in the next generation in Kant's thesis that beauty is nothing but the symbol of the morally good.

V

With the disappearance of Ecclesia and Synagoga from Christian imagery in the sixteenth century, this study is concluded. In allegorical figures Christian doctrine there confronted her predecessor and rival in the belief in one God. This confrontation remained primarily dialogue among Christians in hymns, sermons, and works of art in order to arrive at self-understanding. The prefiguration of the two allegories in the Old Testament—in the Lamentations of Jeremiah and the Proverbs of Solomon—does not at all change the Christian character of this dialogue. The Jewish interpretation of these passages, as similar as it might appear from time to time, was no more taken into account than were the Jewish exegeses of scripture generally. Christianity, beginning with St. Paul, had taken possession of the entire Old Testament, the religious heritage of Judaism, and had interpreted it to suit its own purposes. The allegory became a weapon and instrument of conversion. Inherent in the monologue was the contentious dialogue.

A dialogue between partners was possible only under the influence of *Concordia*. This opportunity presented itself in the Arian confession and also in the accidental historical vacuum of a transitional period, as seen in the dialogue between Gregory of Tours and Priscus (Chapter 5). The Carolingian Renaissance translated *Concordia* into cultural life; there began the artistic representation of the two allegories (Chapter 1) that culminated in the great symbols of concord (Chapter 10). It was the silent, mutual recognition of the sisters in the face of the last judgment and was in complete contrast to the tendencies of the times. This was true also of the Christian humanism of Johann Reuchlin and of Dante, who helped pre-Christian *Humanitas* acquire religious recognition.

The prerequisite for a dialogue between equals was not given until the eighteenth century with the emancipation of the Jews; in "the morning breeze of freedom," as Moses Mendelssohn called it, this dialogue at once got underway, as evidenced in the works of Lessing or the correspondence between Mendelssohn and Lavater, to cite only a few examples. But this mutual recognition found itself exposed to a quickly changing world. Political upheavels were followed by social revolutions, which did not come to a standstill even after industrialization had brought about a complete restructuring of society. At the same time, secularization of religion, a legacy from the Enlightenment, took hold of both Judaism and Christianity and plunged them into severe internal crises. Into the religious vacuum of the nineteenth century and the turn of the century stepped the idolization of social forces, of the state, and of money.

Events in our very recent past have again provided a vivid reminder of the religious roots of life and the still unresolved "religious conflict." Religious dialogues are held in terms of existentialism and are reflected in contemporary literature, which is much too numerous to be specified. We shall mention here only the names of Martin Buber, Franz Werfel, Romano Guardini, Gertrud von Le Fort, Wilhelm Maurer, and Hans

Joachim Schoeps.[7] There is a searching for understanding on a higher level, "a third one—namely the spirit and truth in which all religions have had their origins" (H. J. Schoeps).

For we are no longer dealing with Christianity or Judaism alone, but with belief in the one God who has revealed himself to all men—with that religion that Blaise Pascal tried to show was common to both true Jews and true Christians (Fragment 610).

List of Illustrations

Figure 1
Letter *O* from Drogo's Sacramentary: Ecclesia beneath the cross. Ca. 850; out of workshop in Metz. Ms. Latinus 9428, Bibliothèque Nationale, Paris. Courtesy of the Bibliothèque Nationale, Paris.

Figure 2
Nikasius diptych (detail): Ecclesia and Synagoga beneath the cross. Ca. 900. Treasury, Notre Dame cathedral, Tournai. Courtesy of Bildarchiv Foto Marburg, Marburg.

Figure 3
Tablet: Ecclesia and Synagoga beneath the cross. Ivory. Ninth century; out of workshop in Metz. No. 250.67, Victoria and Albert Museum, London. Courtesy of the Victoria and Albert Museum, London.

Figure 4
Adalbero's tablet: Ecclesia and Synagoga beneath the cross. Ivory. Ca. 1000; out of workshop in Metz. Musées de Metz, Metz. Courtesy of Musèes de Metz, Metz.

Figure 5
Book cover of the Bamberg evangelistary: Ecclesia beneath the cross and in disputation with Synagoga. Ivory. Ca. 870. Codex

Latinus 4452, Staatsbibliothek, Munich. Courtesy of Bildarchiv Foto Marburg, Marburg.

Figure 6
Book cover of the Metz evangelistary: Mary and John beneath the cross; Ecclesia in disputation with Synagoga. Ivory. Ca. 900; out of workshop in Metz. Codex Latinus 9383, Bibliothèque Nationale, Paris. Courtesy of Bildarchiv Foto Marburg, Marburg.

Figure 7
Tablet: Ecclesia beneath the cross; Synagoga fleeing. Ivory. Ca. 900. Museo Nazionale (Bargello), Florence. Courtesy of Museo Nazionale (Bargello), Florence.

Figures 8 and 9
Medallions from the cross of Gunhilde of Denmark: Ecclesia and Synagoga. Ivory. Ca. 1075. Museet Nationale, Copenhagen. Courtesy of Museet Nationale, Copenhagen.

Figure 10
Miniature in the Uta evangelistary: crucifixion with allegories of Life and Death; Ecclesia in the left border and Synagoga in the right. Early eleventh century; out of workshop in Regensburg. Codex Latinus 13601, Staatsbibliothek, Munich. Courtesy of Bildarchiv Foto Marburg, Marburg.

Figure 11
Tablet: one angel directing Ecclesia and another driving Synagoga away. Ivory. Eleventh century; from lower Italy. Staatliche Museen, Berlin-Dahlem. Courtesy of Staatliche Museen, Berlin-Dahlem.

Figure 12
Tablet: Mary and Ecclesia beneath the cross; Ecclesia holding a five-leaf branch instead of a chalice; Synagoga, holding hyssop branch, and John. Ivory. Early eleventh century; from Liège. Treasury, cathedral, Tongern. Courtesy of Institut Royal du Patrimoine Artistique, Brussels.

Figure 13
Tablet: Mary and Ecclesia; Synagoga, holding hyssop branch, and John, beneath the cross. Ivory. Early eleventh century; from Liège. Institut Royal du Patrimoine Artistique, Brussels. Courtesy of Institut Royal du Patrimoine Artistique, Brussels.

Figure 14
Tablet: crucifixion scene with Ecclesia and Mary, John and Synagoga. Ivory. Ca. 1050; from Cologne. Hessisches Landesmuseum, Darmstadt. Courtesy of Hessisches Landesmuseum, Darmstadt.

Figure 15
Head of Moses (detail). Ca. 1405; by Claus Sluter. Moses-fountain, Chartreuse de Champmol, Dijon. Courtesy of Kösel-Verlag, Munich.

Figure 16
Moses. Ca. 1515; by Michelangelo. Tomb of Pope Julius II, San Pietro in Vincoli, Rome. Courtesy of Kösel-Verlag, Munich.

Figure 17
Woodcut from *The Little Passion: The Annunciation.* Ca. 1510; by Albrecht Dürer. Photograph by W. Seiferth.

Figure 18
Illustration in missal: allegory of the sacrifice of the mass; Synagoga piercing the lamb, the spear breaking in her hand, and Ecclesia receiving the blood. Before 1250; from Noyon. Collection of Mr. and Mrs. Philip Hofer, The Walters Art Gallery, Baltimore, Maryland. Courtesy of The Walters Art Gallery, Collection of Mr. and Mrs. Philip Hofer, Baltimore, Maryland.

Figure 19
Detail of window: Synagoga fainting in Aaron's arms; St. Peter crowning the victorious Ecclesia. Late twelfth century. Cathedral, Le Mans. Reproduced from Cahier and Martin.

Figure 20
Detail of passion window: Ecclesia as victorious queen with the church and the tree of life; a devil shooting an arrow into Synagoga's eye. Early thirteenth century. Cathedral, Chartres. Reproduced from Cahier and Martin.

Figure 21
Rim design on paten: Jews approaching hell. Silver. Ca. 1160; from convent in Wilten, Tyrol. Kunsthistorisches Museum, Vienna. Courtesy of Kunsthistorisches Museum, Vienna.

Figure 30
Window detail: Crucifixion scene with Ecclesia and Synagoga (from a copy; incorrectly restored with Synagoga carrying a purse instead of a goat's head). Thirteenth century. Leben-Jesu window, St. Kunibert, Cologne. Photograph by W. Seiferth.

Figure 31
First medallion in window of Suger: Christ crowning Ecclesia and removing Synagoga's blindfold. Middle of twelfth century. Abbey church of St. Denis, Paris. Reproduced from Cahier and Martin.

Figures 32, 33, and 34
Statues: Ecclesia and Synagoga. 1230–40. Formerly at the Prince's Portal and now in the ambulatory, cathedral, Bamberg. Courtesy of Deutscher Kunstverlag, Munich.

Figures 35, 36, and 37
Statues: Ecclesia and Synagoga. 1230–40. South façade of transept, cathedral, Strasbourg. 35 and 37 are courtesy of Bildarchiv Foto Marburg, Marburg. 36 is reproduced from Dehio.

Figure 38
Statue: Synagoga with an empty, downward-turned oil jar (symbol of the foolish virgins). 1247. Shrine of St. Eleutherius, cathedral, Tournai. Courtesy of Institut Royal du Patrimoine Artistique, Brussels.

Figure 39
Statues: Prince of the World and three foolish virgins. Middle of the thirteenth century. West portal, cathedral, Strasbourg. Courtesy of Bildarchiv Foto Marburg, Marburg.

Figure 40
Statues: Prince of the World, Lust with a goat's head, and the angel of warning. Early fourteenth century. Narthex, cathedral, Freiburg. Courtesy of Bildarchiv Foto Marburg, Marburg.

Figure 41
Baptismal font: Three foolish virgins with broken flagstaff and a goat's head (symbols of Synagoga). 1337; by Hans Apengeter. Marienkirche, Lübeck. Courtesy of Photo-Atelier Castelli, Lübeck.

Figure 42
Side of choir stall: Synagoga. 1284; by Master of Duderstadt, Pöhlde monastery. Niedersächsische Landesgalerie, Hanover. Courtesy of Niedersächsische Landesgalerie, Hanover.

Figure 43
Shrine of St. Lomer: Ecclesia. Repoussé in copper and gold. Late twelfth century. Puy-de-Dôme, Moissat-Bas, Auvergne. Photograph by W. Seiferth.

Figure 44
Miniature: Ecclesia Universalis receiving the book of Genesis from Moses's hand. Ca. 1000. Title page of the Bernward Bible, Hildesheim. Reproduced from Goldschmidt, *Buchmalerei.*

Figure 45
Miniature: triumph of the church; Ecclesia sharing the throne of the world with Christ. Second half of the thirteenth century; German master. Rosenwald Collection, The National Gallery of Art, Washington, D.C. Courtesy of The National Gallery of Art, Rosenwald Collection, Washington, D.C.

Figure 46
Statue: the so-called "little Ecclesia." Middle of the thirteenth century; out of the same workshop as figures 35, 36, and 37. Cathedral museum, Strasbourg. Courtesy of Bildarchiv Foto Marburg, Marburg.

Figure 47
Miniature: Ecclesia on the second day of creation. Thirteenth century. Codex Fr. 9561, folio 3, Bibliothèque Nationale, Paris. Courtesy of Bibliothèque Nationale, Paris.

Figure 48
Miniature: God uniting the hands of Adam and Eve; Christ wedding Ecclesia. Thirteenth century. Codex Fr. 9561, folio 8, Bibliothèque Nationale, Paris. Courtesy of Bibliothèque Nationale, Paris.

Figure 49
Miniature: Birth of Ecclesia at the death of Christ; creation of Eve; a child's baptism (beneath the cross at the left); Moses with the tablets of stone (beneath the cross at the right). Ca. 1250. Codex Latinus 11560, folio 186, Bibliothèque Nationale, Paris. Courtesy of Bibliothèque Nationale, Paris.

Figure 50
Miniature: Ecclesia between Suffering, interpreted as the death of a martyr (at the left), and Passion, interpreted as a love scene (at the right). Ca. 1410; out of the workshop of the brothers of Limburg. Codex Fr. 166, folio 1, Bibliothèque Nationale, Paris. Courtesy of Bibliothèque Nationale, Paris.

Figure 51
Miniature: the heavenly couple, Christ and Ecclesia. Ca. 1230; from a series of miniatures of the Revelation of St. John. Pierpont Morgan Library, New York. Courtesy of Pierpont Morgan Library, New York.

Figure 52
Miniature: Burial of Synagoga. Ca. 1410; out of the workshop of the brothers of Limburg. Codex Fr. 166, folio 40 v, Bibliothèque Nationale, Paris. Courtesy of Bibliothèque Nationale, Paris.

Figure 53
Miniature: Ecclesia witnessing the birth of Christ through the opened curtain. Ca. 1250. Codex Latinus 11560, folio 202, Bibliothèque Nationale, Paris. Courtesy of Bibliothèque Nationale, Paris.

Figure 54
Miniature: Ecclesia with the tablets of the Old Testament; Mary with the Christ Child; the Duke of Burgundy, donor, with his retinue. Ca. 1410; out of the workshop of the brothers of Limburg. Codex Fr. 166, folio 46, Bibliothèque Nationale, Paris. Courtesy of Bibliothèque Nationale, Paris.

Figure 55
Relief: Ecclesia holding a candelabra and witnessing the birth of Christ. Early fourteenth century. Tympanum above the narthex, cathedral, Freiburg. Courtesy of Bildarchiv Foto Marburg, Marburg.

Figure 56
Painting (detail): Ecclesia Universalis, the so-called "Mary before the time." Ca. 1515; from the Isenheimer altar by Mathis Grünewald. Museum, Colmar. Courtesy of Kösel-Verlag, Munich.

Figure 57
Fresco (detail): the creation of Adam; Eve, the type of Ecclesia

Universalis, peering from under the arm of God the Creator. Ca. 1510; by Michelangelo. Ceiling of the Sistine Chapel, Rome. Courtesy of Kösel-Verlag, Munich.

Figure 58
Wood painting: Synagoga. Ca. 1430; by Konrad Witz. Kunstmuseum, Basel. Courtesy of Kunstmuseum, Basel.

Figure 59
Initial *A*: Presentation of the "living cross"; Ecclesia as madonna of the protective mantle. Late fifteenth century. Codex Monacensis 23041, folio 3 v, Staatsbibliothek, Munich. Courtesy of Staatsbibliothek, Munich.

Figure 60
Frontispiece from *Dialogus de diversarum gentium sectis et mundi religionibus;* published by Johannes Stamler, Augsburg: Ecclesia with pope and emperor; disputation of Doctor Oliverus. 1508; workshop of Hans Burgkmair, Augsburg. Photograph by W. Seiferth.

Figures 61 and 62
Woodcuts: prostitutes of the lansquenets taking the place of the foolish virgins (one of the final versions). 1518, by Nikolaus Manuel Deutsch. Photographs by W. Seiferth.

Figure 63
Copper engraving: Venus taking the place of one of the foolish virgins (one of the final versions). 1513, by Urs Graf. Photograph by W. Seiferth.

Figure 64
Relief: Baptism of a Jew. Ca. 1220. Baptismal font of the parish church, Lippoldsberg on the Weser. Courtesy of Evangelische Pfarrkirche, Lippoldsberg.

Figure 65
Medallion from the cross of Bury St. Edmunds: Synagoga with a broken spear, and the lamb of God; on the right is an angel, and beneath the lamb is Jeremiah; behind Synagoga St. John is mourning. Ivory. Late twelfth century. The Metropolitan Museum of Art, The Cloisters Collection, New York. Courtesy of The Metropolitan Museum of Art, The Cloisters Collection, New York.

1

2

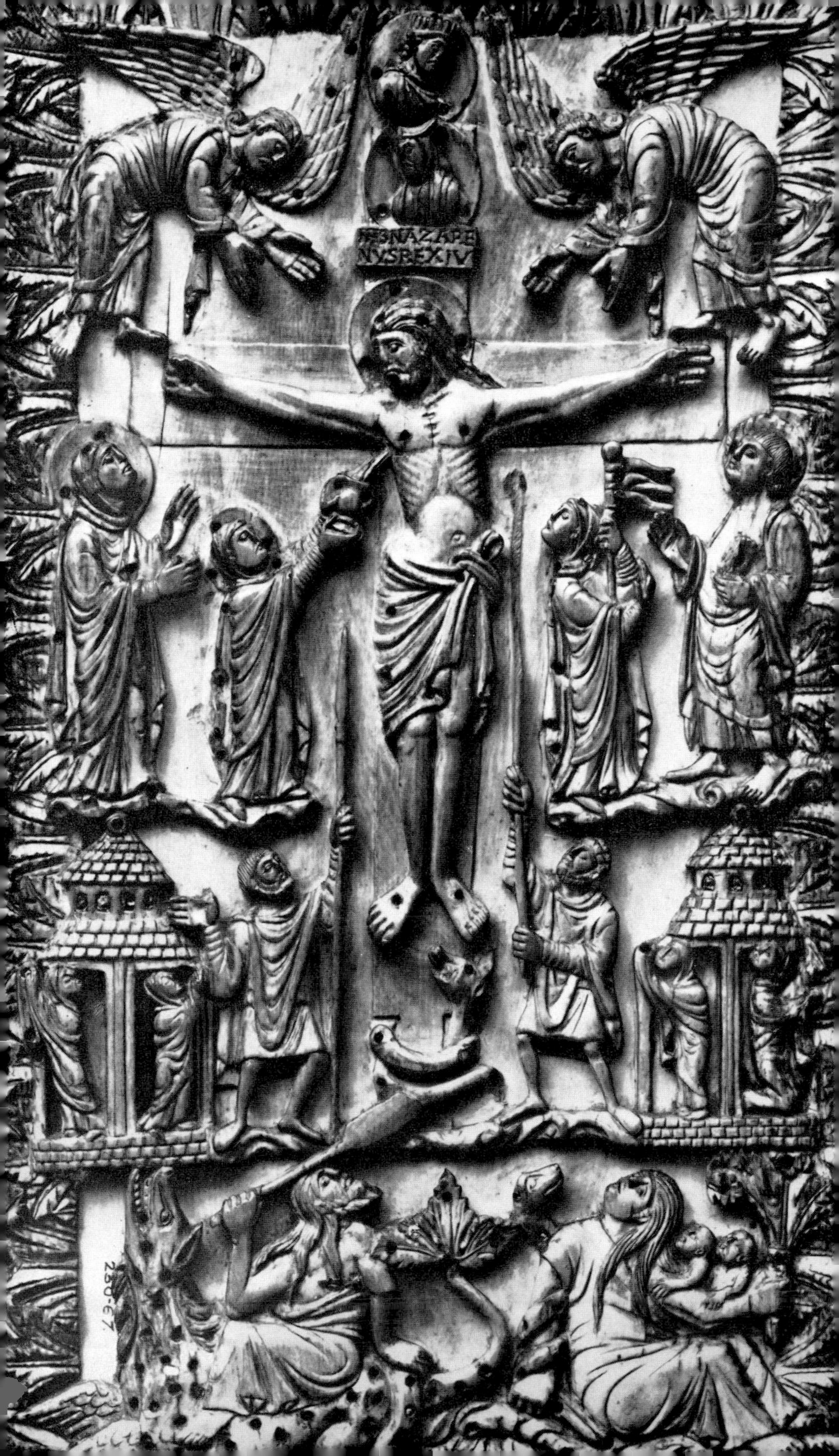

IHSNAZARE
NVSREXIV
230-67

4

6

7 8 9

LVNA
STEFA

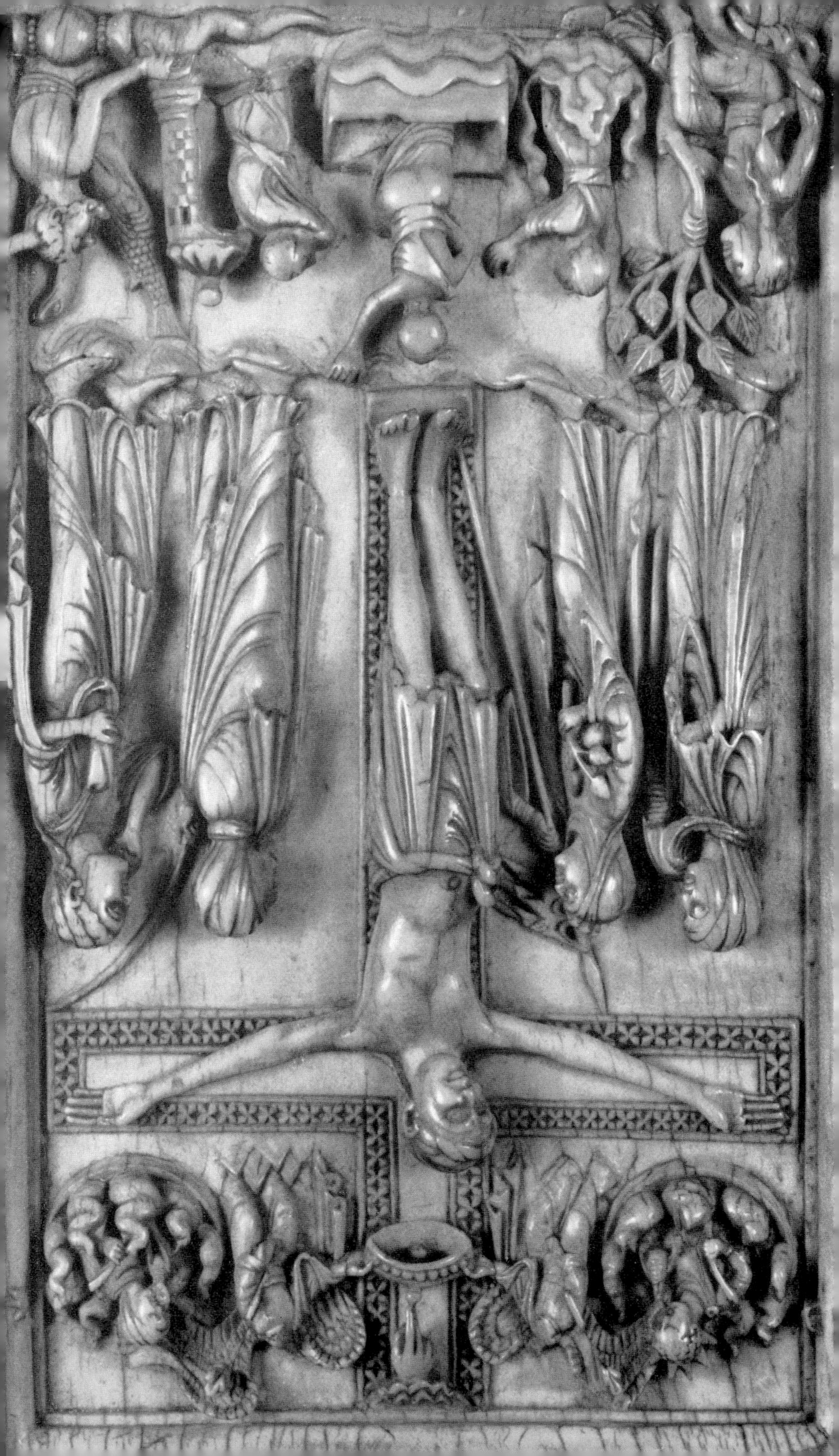

4

15

16

17

18

19

20

ysaias p̄cinit s̄nagoga meminit nūqm̄ tam̄ desinit eē
ceca. s̄nagaga imitat' eccl̄ia.

23

22

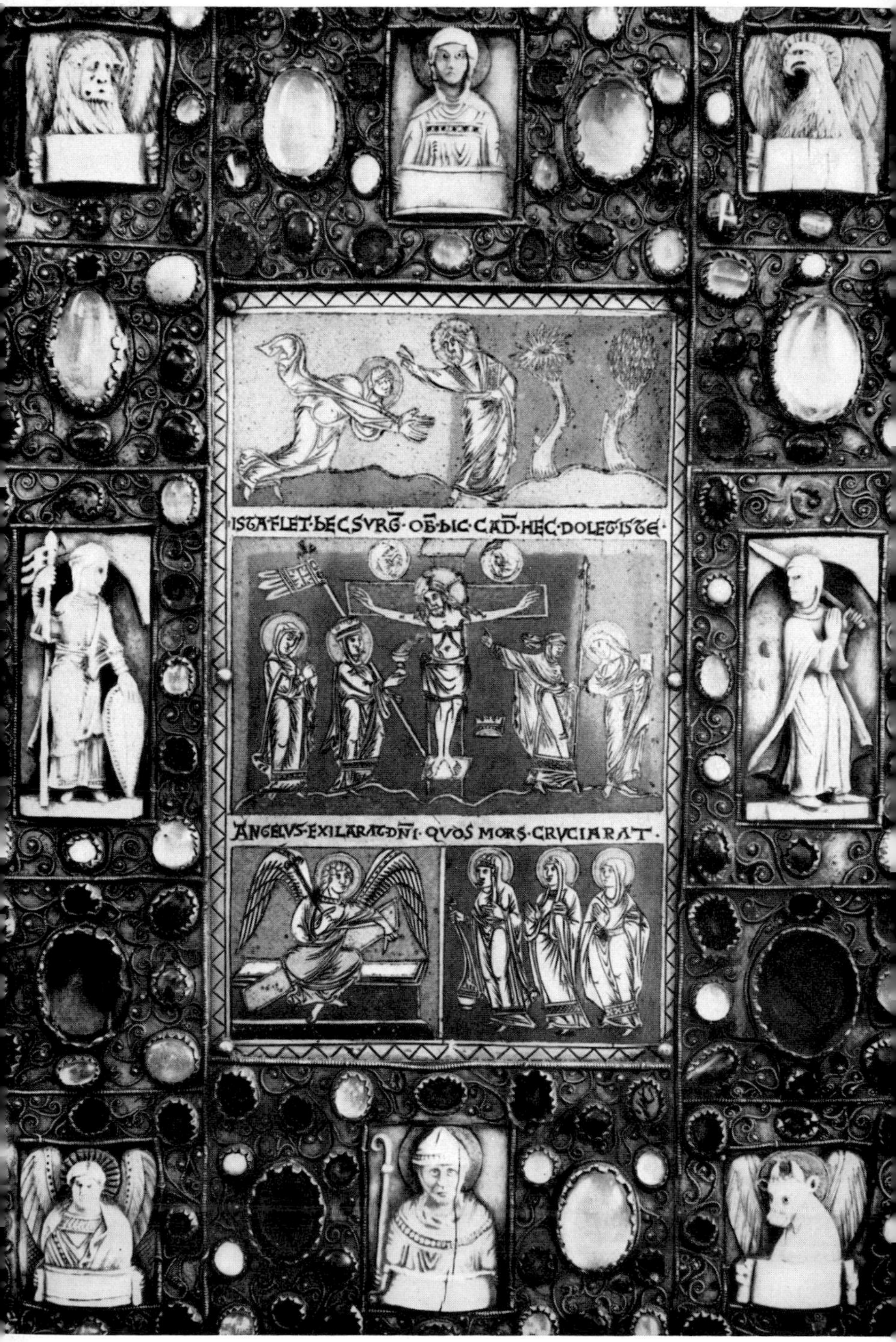

ISTA FLET·HEC SVRG̅·OB·HIC·CAD̅·HEC·DOLET·ISTE·
ANGELVS·EXILARAT·DN̅I·QVOS MORS·CRVCIARAT·

24

IHC. NAZARENVS.
REX. IVDEORVM.
FODERERVNT MANVS MEAS.
DIXI. ASCENDAM. IN PALMAM.

25

26

27

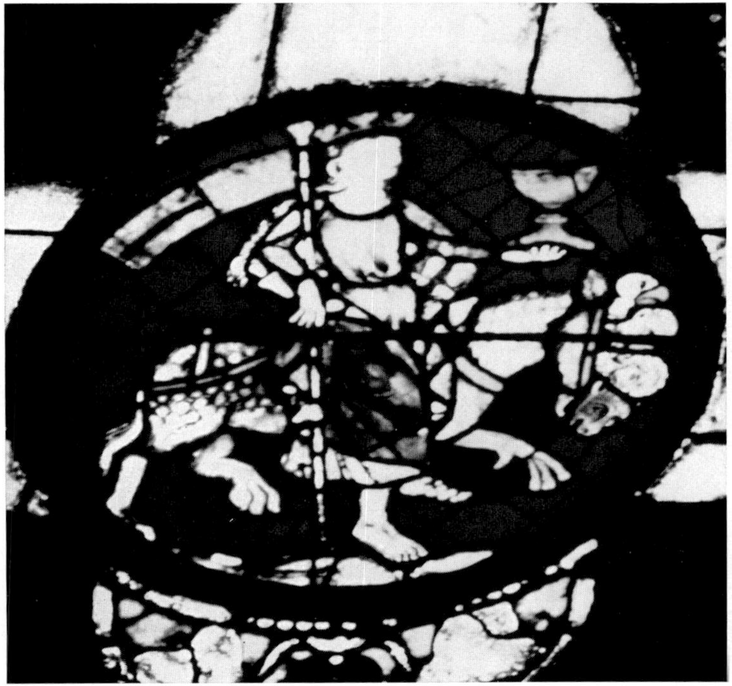

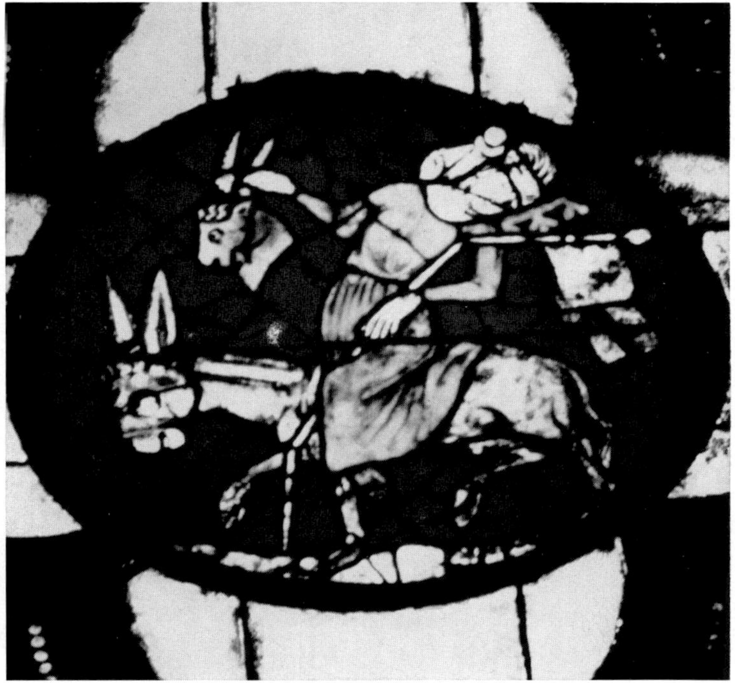

28

30

31

32

33

34

35

36

37

38

39

40

41 42 43

45

46

47

48

49

50

51

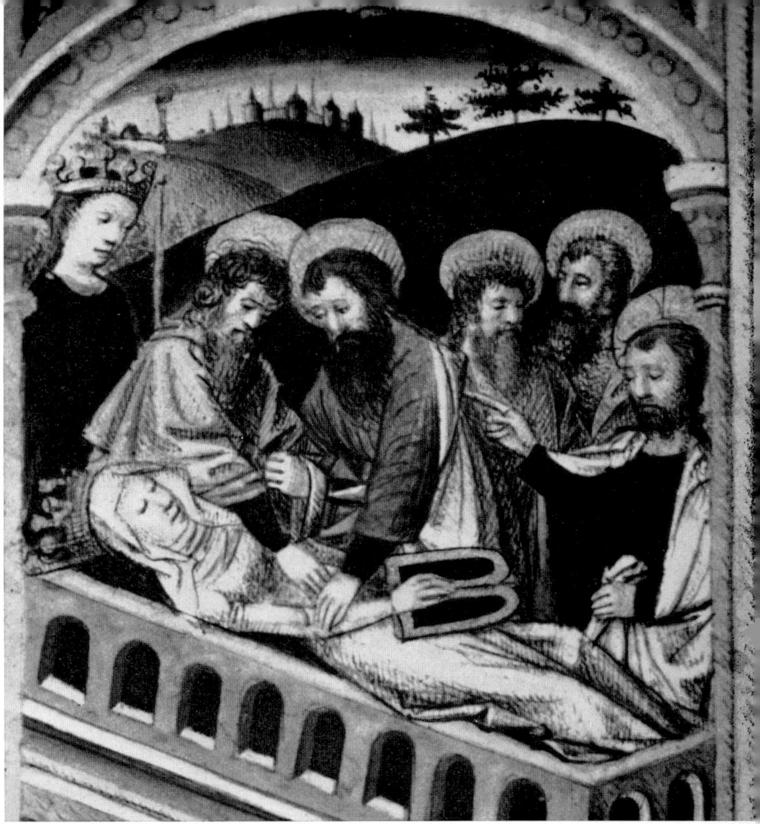

52

53

54

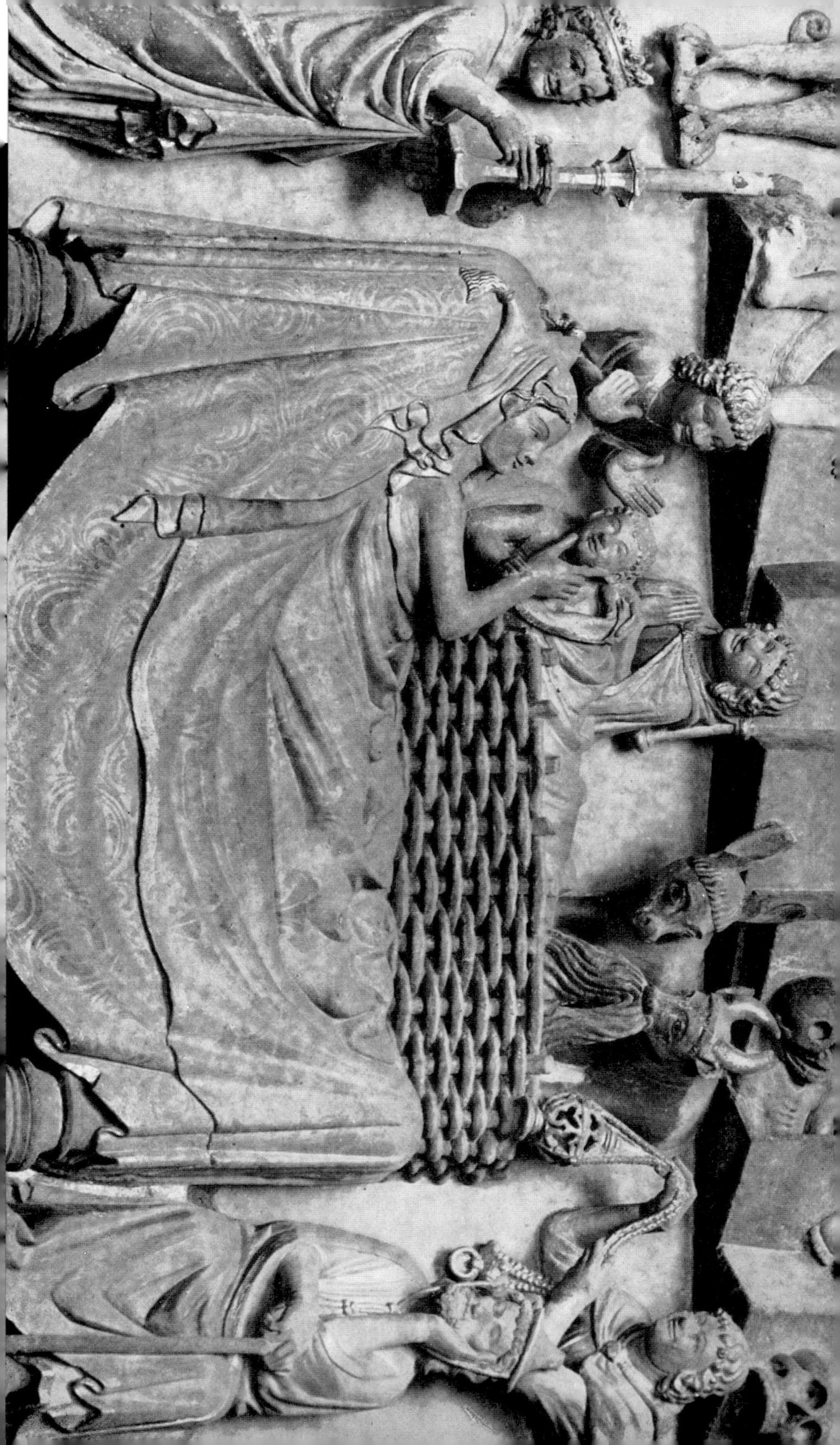

58

DYALOGUS·IOHANNIS STAMLER·AUGUSTN.
DE DIVERSARUM GENCIUM SECTIS
ET MUNDI RELIGIONIBUS
IHS
SOLA
SANCTA·MATER·ECCLESIA
INRI
ORA·ET·CURA
PROTEGE
IMPPERA
MACHOMETUS
IUPITER
CHINGISTA
FONS·VERE SAPIENCE
IUSTA·EST RELIGIO
SINAGOGA
SARACENATHUR
GENTILITAS
S. TARTARICA
DISPUTATORES
Doctor Oliueri9
Balbus historicus
Triphon phisic9
I S
H B
Rudolph9 laic9
Samuel Iudeus
Arnestes Apostota
Registru operis respice in fine

61
62
63

64

Notes

Chapter 1

1 Group A, consisting of the following ivory tablets all dating from the ninth or tenth century: book cover of the Codex Latinus 9453, Bibliothèque Nationale, Paris (Goldschmidt I, No. 86); book cover in the parish church of St. Croix, Departement Allier, Gannat (Goldschmidt I, No. 89); tablet No. 250.67, Victoria and Albert Museum, London (Goldschmidt I, No. 85; Fig. 3); tablet of Adalbero, Musées de Metz, Metz (Goldschmidt I, No. 75; Fig. 4).

2 Group B, consisting of the following ivory tablets: book cover of the Bamberg evangelistary, Codex Latinus 4452, Staatsbibliothek, Munich (Goldschmidt I, No. 41; Fig. 5); book cover of the Codex Latinus 9383, Bibliothèque Nationale, Paris (Goldschmidt I, No. 83; Fig. 6); ivory tablet No. 266.67, Victoria and Albert Museum, London (Goldschmidt I, No. 132a).

3 No. 252–67, Victoria and Albert Museum (Goldschmidt II, No. 67).

4 Miniature in the Uta evangelistary, composed about 1050 in Regensburg; Codex Latinus 13601, Staatsbibliothek, Munich.

5 Formerly in the Kaiser Friedrich Museum, and now in the Staatliche Museen, Berlin-Dahlem.

6 Cathedral treasury, Tongern (Goldschmidt II, No. 57; Fig. 12); Institut Royal du Patrimoine Artistique, Brussels (Goldschmidt II, No. 55; Fig. 13); book cover of Theophano, treasury of the Monastery of Essen (Goldschmidt II, No. 58).

7 Hessisches Landes-Museum, Darmstadt (Goldschmidt II, No. 59).

Chapter 2

1 For example, in the *Hortus Deliciarum* of Herrad von Landsberg, twelfth century.

2 Quoted in A. von Harnack, *Augustin: Reflexionen und Maximen.*

3 Quoted (in German translation) in P. Weber, *Geistliches Schauspiel und kirchliche Kunst.* Early Christian art often expressed this thought, most memorably in the mosaics of Santa Pudenciana and Santa Sabina in Rome.

4 From the Corpus Christi Sequence of Thomas Aquinas, "Lauda, Sion Salvatorem" (K. Langosch, *Hymnen*, No. 70).

5 A hidden but consequential Old Testament source of typology is found in Ecclesiastes 1:9–10, enphasizing the unchangeable structure of man's life and the highest characteristic of the Eternal: "What has been is what will be, and what has been done is what will be done; and there is nothing new under the sun."

6 Quoted in H. J. Schoeps, *Jüdische Geisteswelt*, p. 64.

7 Especially recommended is F. X. Kraus, *Geschichte der christlichen Kunst*, II, 271.

8 Quoted in C. Cahier and A. Martin, *Vitraux peints*, I, 66. Even Michelangelo's statues of Rachel and Leah, intended for the grave of Pope Julius II, seem to preserve this contrast of character, although it is masked by the traditional characterizations "active life" and "contemplative life."

9 This was true in the teachings of Hugo von Sankt Viktor (died 1141), the German mystic who taught in Paris and whose ideas were influenced by Gregory the Great. Quoted in H. Reiners and W. Ewald, *Kunstdenkmäler*, Nos. 128 and 139.

10 See J. Klausner, *Jesus von Nazareth.*

Chapter 3

1 The Ambrosian liturgy for Holy Saturday. Quoted (in German translation) in P. Weber, *Geistliches Schauspiel*, Chap. 5.

2 *Opera*, Pars. 1, V, 5. Quoted (in German translation) in P. Weber, *Geistliches Schauspiel*, Chap. 5.
3 It can also be found in other churches in Lorraine; for example, in Metz (the cathedral) and Avioth.
4 H. Reiners and W. Ewald, *Kunstdenkmäler*, p. 138.
5 C. Cahier and A. Martin, *Vitraux peints*, I, 56 ff.
6 Sedulius, *Carmina*, V, 357. The translation is based on the text in F. X. Kraus, *Geschichte*, II, 344.
7 From the translation of F. J. Mone, *Hymnen*, I, Nos. 154 and 160.
8 K. Langosch, *Hymnen*, No. 71. The complete German translation of this sequence is in G. Pfannmüller, *Jesus*, p. 178.
9 J. P. Migne, *Patrologia Latina*, Vol. LIV (*De Passione Domini*). From the German translation of T. Steeger, *Sermone*.
10 Text in J. P. Migne, *Patrologia Latina*, XLII, 1131–40 (appendix of Augustine's *De Altercatione Ecclesiae et Synagogae Dialogus*).

Chapter 4

1 P. Weber, *Geistliches Schauspiel*.
2 From the Latin text in J. P. Migne, *Patrologia Latina*, XLII, 1123 ff.

Chapter 5

1 H. J. Schoeps, in *Religionsgespräch*, Chap. 18, even speaks of the "bitter struggle between Judaism and Christianity for religious dominance."
2 Quoted in J. Bühler, *Die Germanen in der Völkerwanderung*, p. 280.
3 I. von Döllinger, *Die Juden in Europa*.
4 *Historia Francorum*, VI, 5.
5 See P. Weber, *Geistliches Schauspiel*, Chap. 6.
6 Similar situations occurred in Spain in the fifteenth century and were the grounds for the expulsion of the Jews in 1492. The general edict on the expulsion is reprinted in H. J. Schoeps, *Jüdische Geisteswelt*, pp. 153–57.

Chapter 6

1 *Verantwortung* (Kösel Verlag, Munich, 1952), p. 27.

2 Text in *Monumenta Germaniae historica: Epistolae Karolingi Aevi*, Tom. III, 1899 (J. P. Migne, *Patrologia Latina*, LIV). Concerning Agobard, see T. A. Cabaniss, *Agobard of Lyon*, and B. Gebhardt, *Handbuch der deutschen Geschichte*, I, 44.

Chapter 7

1 Quoted in H. J. Schoeps, *Jüdische Geisteswelt*, p. 142. See also S. W. Baron, *History*, II, 32 ff.
2 "Eckehard of Aura and the Saxon Annalist," quoted in J. Bühler, *Die Sächsischen und Salischen Kaiser*, pp. 343 ff. Similar passages are in H. J. Schoeps, *Jüdische Geisteswelt*, pp. 142–49.
3 Quoted in L. Zunz, *Die synagogale Poesie*, p. 16. Cf. H. G. Adler, *Die Juden in Deutschland*, pp. 69 ff.
4 "Deeds of the Bishops of Trier," quoted in J. Bühler, *Die Sächsischen und Salischen Kaiser*, pp. 344–45.
5 In addition to various taxes that the Jews had to pay yearly to the emperor, they had to transfer a third of their wealth to the Roman kings and emperors after the election of each king and the crowning of each emperor, for the "mercy" of not being burned to death, which the king and the emperor had the "right" to do. See J. Bühler, *Fürsten und Ritter*, p. 405. See also H. G. Adler, *Die Juden in Deutschland*, pp. 24–26, and Old German Jewish oaths in Müllenhoff-Scherer, *Denkmäler*, pp. 625 ff.
6 For example, the pointed hat, which is portrayed even at an earlier date than this (see Chapter 9). In the illustrated Heidelberg manuscript of the *Sachsenspiegel*, an early Saxon code of laws, the hat denotes the exceptional legal position of the Jews.
7 See J. Bühler, *Die Hohenstaufen*, p. 424 (*Jahrbücher von Marbach, 1236*). See also *Des Knaben Wunderhorn*, a collection of German folk songs (reprint of the Heidelberg edition of 1819; Meersburg, 1928), I, 93–96.
8 For information about the events of 1349, see the following: the chronicle of J. von Königshofen; J. Bühler, *Bauern, Bürger und Hansa, nach zeitgenössischen Quellen*, pp. 134–38; J. Nohl, *Der schwarze Tod* (Potsdam, 1924), Chap. 7.
9 Epistola 363, 6 (in J. P. Migne, *Patrologia Latina*, CLXXXII, 564). See also D. Baumgardt, *Great Western Mystics*.
10 *Berthold von Regensburgs Deutsche Predigten*, translated into modern German and introduced by O. H. Brandt (Jena, 1924), No. 42.

11 Also expressed in the *Sachsenspiegel.* See also the illustrations, especially Plate 83, in the Heidelberg manuscript of the *Sachsenspiegel.*

12 Quoted in W. Vesper, *Der deutsche Psalter*, p. 72.

13 Quoted in G. Liebe, *Das Judentum in der deutschen Vergangenheit*, p. 67.

Chapter 8

1 See K. Langosch, *Geistliche Spiele*, pp. 100 ff. and 245 ff.

2 *De investigatione Antichristi* (ca. 1161). See R. Froning, "Das Drama des Mittelalters" in *Deutsche Nationalliteratur*, Vol. XIV; also *Gerhohi Opera*, Scheibelberger, ed. (Linz, 1875), I, 26.

3 The latest edition of the *Ludus* appears in K. Langosch, *Geistliche Spiele;* older editions are in R. Froning and W. Meyer. English is in S. F. Barrow and W. H. Hulme, "Antichrist and Adam," *Western Reserve University Bulletin* (Cleveland, 1925).

4 Gerhoh von Reichersberg lived at precisely the same time as the author of the *Ludus.* Perhaps Gerhoh's objections refer directly to this antichrist play, although it appears doubtful that it could have been performed by the clergy alone.

5 This quotation from the *Ludus*, as well as those following, are taken from S. F. Barrow and W. H. Hulme, "Antichrist and Adam," *Western Reserve University Bulletin.*

6 From the outset and throughout the play, Synagoga wears a blindfold over her eyes.

7 *Hypocrisis* does not suggest conscious insincerity as much as it does self-deception.

8 As suggested by W. Michaelis, "Zum Ludus de Antichristo" in *Zeitschrift für deutsches Altertum.*

9 See also H. J. Schoeps, *Religionsgespräch*, Chap. 4.

10 Quoted in German translation in K. Langosch, *Geistliche Spiele.* See also W. Creizenach, *Geschichte des neueren Dramas*, I, 90.

11 See K. Langosch, *Geistliche Spiele*, pp. 248 and 263. The third portion of the *Christmas Play of Benediktbeuren* is printed in K. Young, *The Drama of the Mediaeval Church*, II, 463 ff.

12 See J. Sauer, *Symbolik*, p. 257.

13 W. Creizenach, *Geschichte des neueren Dramas*, I, 125. Also, Heym, in *Zeitschrift für deutsches Altertum*, LII, 1 ff.

14 Cf. Chapter 12, pp. 142–43.

Chapter 9

1 Cf. Chapter 7.

2 Quoted in the edition of W. Pfeiffer-Bartsch (Leipzig, 1911), No. 87.

3 J. Sauer, *Symbolik*, p. 259. For a systematic classification of the numerous examples of Ecclesia and Synagoga in the twelfth and thirteenth centuries, see the iconographic handbooks of H. Bergner, H. Detzel, K. Künstle, W. Molsdorf, D. Otte, J. Sauer, and others.

4 Cf. Chapter 7.

5 Codex D4, folio 8b. Cf. W. Molsdorf, *Christliche Symbolik*, p. 179; also J. Sauer, *Symbolik*, p. 254.

6 The identification of Synagoga with the Jewish community reaches its highpoint in the Tucher window in the Freiburg Cathedral (after 1300)—Synagoga in the yellow garment of the Jewess. C. Cahier and A. Martin pointed out long ago—without perceiving the connection with the crusades—that soon thereafter many documents of church art no longer viewed Synagoga as representing the Old Testament doctrine but representing, rather, medieval Jewry, which seemed to blaspheme this doctrine. Cf. bibliography.

7 Middle of the twelfth century; now in the museum there. Cf. J. Sauer, *Symbolik*, p. 157.

8 J. Sauer, *Symbolik*, p. 255. The picture is lost.

9 Illustration in the missal of Noyon (before 1250), Walters Art Gallery, Baltimore, Maryland.

10 The cross of Bury St. Edmunds was for many years in private hands and not, consequently, available for study and research. In 1963, however, since the cross was purchased by the Metropolitan Museum of Art in New York for display in the Cloisters Collection, it has become accessible to the public.

For further information about the cross, see Thomas P. Hoving, "The Bury St. Edmunds Cross," in *The Metropolitan Museum of Art Bulletin*, 1964, pp. 317–40 (with thirty-six illustrations). See also "The Ivory Cross of the Collection Topic-Mimara," in *Wallraf-Richartz Jahrbuch*, xxv (1963).

11 As in the *Sachsenspiegel* manuscript and the Manesse manuscript (of courtly medieval love poetry)—both of which are in Heidelberg.

12 Codex a, XII, 7, Stiftsbibliothek, Salzburg.

13 As suggested by E. Mâle, *L'art*, p. 193.
14 Codex 108, folio 43a.
15 Quoted in A. Schmarsow, *Italienische Kunst im Zeitalter Dantes.*
16 No. 13068. A primitive copy can be found in the Museum of Fine Arts, Boston, No. 59,518.
17 H. Swarzenski, *Vorgotische Miniaturen*, p. 62.
18 As they also have in the Helmershausen Sacramentary (between 1160 and 1180; today in the Kestner Museum, Hanover) among others.
19 De Sacr. Alt. 31, quoted in J. Sauer, *Symbolik*, p. 248.
20 E. Mâle, *L'art*, p. 364.
21 Cf. H. Sedlmayr, *Die Entstehung der Kathedrale.*
22 Quoted in E. Mâle, *L'art.*
23 The chancel of the abbey church of St. Denis was dedicated in 1144. It is uncertain whether the windows were completed at that time or not. Bernard's sermon (cf. Chapter 7) was given in the year 1148. The *Ludus* is usually placed in the first years of the reign of Frederick Barbarossa, i.e., soon after 1152.

Also in the tradition of the Suger window is the baptismal font in the Bibliothèque Municipale, Amiens (twelfth century), which repeats the motif of the veil that is to be lifted. See J. Sauer, *Symbolik*, p. 249; also W. Molsdorf, *Christliche Symbolik*, p. 181 (there misinterpreted). The figure of Synagoga with blindfold and instruments of torture in Châlons-sur-Marne (cf. Chapter 9) is approximately contemporaneous with the window in the chancel of the abbey church of St. Denis.
24 For more information on Suger, see Otto von Simson, *The Gothic Cathedral* (Bollinger Foundation, New York, 1956).
25 Quoted in J. Sauer, *Symbolik*, p. 251.
26 I.e., the chalice with the blood of Christ.
27 These can be found today in the Wallace Museum and the Victoria and Albert Museum, London; Lyons; Vatican Museum; Leningrad. An illustration is in O. Pelka, *Elfenbeine*, p. 178.

Chapter 10

1 T. Haecker, *Vergil, Vater des Abendlandes*, chap. 4.
2 The originals are in the cathedral museum.
3 In "Der Aufbruch" (1913). Reprinted in E. Stadler, *Dichtungen*, pp. 180 ff. Two other poetic endeavors should be mentioned

here: F. Braun, "Ecclesia-Synagoge" (statues at the Cathedral of Strasbourg), in S. Kaznelson, *Jüdisches Schicksal in deutschen Gedichten*, pp. 40 ff. (I am indebted to Mrs. Erna Krauss of Tübingen for this reference); J. Hübner, "Synagoge, Kathedrale von Straßburg," in H. Binde, ed., *Deutsche Lyrik. Gedichte seit 1945* (Stuttgart, 1962), p. 92.

4 In Williram's paraphrase of the Song of Solomon (eleventh century), they are clad "in the garb of innocence" (*veste innocentiae*); see Braune, *Althochdeutsches Lesebuch* (1949), p. 64.

5 Regarding this, see the Jewish typology of the first and sixth commandments equating idolatry with adultery (cf. Chapter 2). The Middle High German *ketzerîe* also has both meanings.

6 The famous "Drama of the Wise and Foolish Maidens," which was performed in the year 1322 in Eisenach and caused the landgrave to doubt the grace of God, is limited essentially to the eschatological interpretation. Cf. W. Golther, *Die Deutsche Dichtung im Mittelalter*, pp. 489 ff.

7 Pulpit of the Siena Cathedral, about 1268, at the Shrine of St. Eleutherius in Tournai (1247). Compare with this the words of Albertus Magnus, which date from the same period and reflect such an interpretation: "it is she who has spilled this very blood."

8 Niedersächsische Landesgalerie, Hanover.

Chapter 11

1 I am indebted to Rabbi Dr. Hugo Schiff, Washington, D.C. for this reference.

2 H. J. Schoeps, *Religionsgespräch*, p. 57.

3 Müllenhoff-Scherer, *Denkmäler*, XXXV, No. 132.

4 German version is in W. Vesper, *Die Ernte der Deutschen Lyrik*, p. 29.

5 Cf. Chapter 2.

6 As in the mosaic on the portal of Santa Sabina in Rome, dating from the fifth century.

7 Herzog-Anton-Ulrich Museum, catalog No. 2.

8 The window in Metz mentioned in Chapter 9, in which Ecclesia is depicted among the prophets, also belongs thematically to this group (in the cathedral, west gable of the north aisle).

9 Codex Sal. IXb, folio 40, Universitätsbibliothek, Heidelberg; reproduced in Goldschmidt, *Die deutsche Buchmalerei*.

10 As in Exultet Rolls, Bibliotheca Barberina, Rome.

11 Cf. *Manuscrits à peintures du XIIIe au XVIe siècle*, Bibliothèque Nationale, Paris (1955), No. 6.

12 Cf. *Catalogue des Manuscrits Français de la Bibliothèque Nationale*, Paris (1896).

13 Cf. *Manuscrits à peintures du XIIIe au XVIe siècle*, No. 147.

14 *Manuscrits à peintures du XIIIe au XVIe siècle*, No. 188.

15 Cf. Chapter 3.

16 This is not the case in the older Codex 11560; it does not begin until the book of Job. Unfortunately, I was not able to examine the complete texts of this manuscript in Toledo and in Vienna.

17 The so-called "Little Ecclesia" in the Cathedral Museum in Strasbourg (Fig. 46) possibly is to be viewed in the same manner: *Ecclesia universalis*, who is present at the creation. The figure originates in the workshop of the great Master of Strasbourg but is rather small in size. It evidently was never used and the context for which it was intended remains in doubt. Dehio imagines the figure to be a Mary of the Annunciation.

18 Cf. in this connection the commentary of Bruno of Segni (died 1123) on Genesis 2: ". . . that the Savior left his heavenly Father and his mother, Synagoga, and that when his side was opened on the cross he entered into close relationship with the church similar to that between Adam and Eve" (J. P. Migne, *Patrologia Latina*, CLXIV, 165 ff.).

19 Cf. the typological value of Leah as Synagoga and Rachel as Ecclesia (Chapter 2, p. 17).

20 An illustration of the line from the "Praise of Solomon"—"she shall bear him the children whom we shall call God's heirs"—is also found in Codex 9561, folio 24v. See in this regard Müllenhoff-Scherer, *Denkmäler*, No. 132.

21 *Mesele* is the Old French for leprosy; cf. English *measles*, German *Masern*, and Middle High German *misele sucht*.

22 Cf. what has been said concerning the *amaritudines mundi* on p. 132.

23 *Ave Maris Stella* 2, translated in K. Langosch, *Hymnen und Vagantenlieder*, p. 24.

24 Both Italian original and English translation in *Dante's Paradiso*, Laurence Binyon, translator (London, 1943).

25 One example of this "interchangeability" has already been given in the so-called "Little Ecclesia" in Strasbourg (Fig. 46) Cf. footnote 17.

26 Pierpont Morgan Library, New York.

27 Codex Fr. 167, folio 46, Bibliothèque Nationale, Paris.

Chapter 12

1 For an extensive discussion, see P. Weber, *Geistliches Schauspiel*, Chaps. 9–12.

2 Second half of the fourteenth century. Text is in R. Froning, ed., *Deutsche Nationalliteratur*, XIV, 2. Cf. also the following: P. Weber, *Geistliches Schauspiel;* W. Creizenach, *Geschichte des neueren Dramas*; and K. Langosch, *Geistliche Spiele.*

3 R. Froning, ed., *Deutsche Nationalliteratur*, XIV, 2.

4 As also in the Künzelsau Corpus Christi play of 1479. Cf. W. Creizenach, *Geschichte des neueren Dramas*, I, 233 ff. Cf. also P. Weber, *Geistliches Schauspiel*, pp. 74 ff.

5 The same is found in a miniature in a German historical Bible, Codex A49, Dresden (ca. 1450) patterned after French-Burgundian miniatures.

6 Quoted in M. F. Modder, *The Jews in the Literature of England to the End of the 19th Century*, p. 16.

7 W. Creizenach, *Geschichte des neueren Dramas*, I, 237 ff.

8 P. Weber, *Geistliches Schauspiel*, p. 129.

9 From 1400 on, the so-called "Jew-pig" is found in churches (in Erfurt, Magdeburg, and elsewhere) in secluded places–for example, under the seats of the canons in the choir.

10 P. Weber lists eleven examples of the "Living Cross" in the Rhineland, Switzerland, and Italy, among them the following: a tablet from the Old Cologne School (ca. 1420), formerly in Sigmaringen; Landshut, portal of St. Mary's Church (ca. 1432); Bologna, fresco in San Petronio (ca. 1440); Beaune (fifteenth century), formerly Musée Cluny, Paris; initial *A*, Codex Monacensis 23041, Munich Staatsbibliothek (end of the fifteenth century); painting by Hans Fries, Freiburg, Switzerland (ca. 1506); fresco in Bruneck, Tyrol (1526); fresco by Garofalo in Ferrara (1532); woodcut in the *Lectiones Memorabiles et Reconditae* by Johann Wolff, Lauingen (1600).

11 In the same Codex Monacensis 23041, this composition is found a second time in folio 181, on a smaller scale and with slight modifications.

12 "On the whole insignificant and repulsive, mere bookish phantasy, but with interesting episodes" (J. Burckhardt, *Cicerone*, 1924, p. 891).

13 One is in the Prado, Madrid, and another is at Oberlin College, Ohio. The latter painting was pointed out to me by Miss Lenore Keene, who was then a student at the College.

14 *Dialogus de diversarum gentium sectis et mundi religionibus* (1508).

Chapter 13

1 Text is in R. Froning, *Drama*, I, 107–98. See also W. Golther, *Die Deutsche Dichtung im Mittelalter*, pp. 491–94.

Chapter 14

1 Cf. E. Benz, *Die christliche Kabbala*, also H. G. Adler, *Die Juden in Deutschland*, p. 27.

2 The author is here indebted to the materials and interpretation given in W. Maurer, *Kirche und Synagoge*, especially in sections 8–10.

3 Region on the border of hell, the abode of the just who died before Christ's coming, Vergil among them (cf. Dante's *Inferno*, Canto 4).

4 Nicolai's hymn remained so popular that as late as 1806 Arnim and Brentano included it in their collection of German folk songs *Des Knaben Wunderhorn*, I, 101 ff.

5 In "Anmutiger Blumenkranz aus dem Garten der Gemeinde Gottes" (1712); also in *Des Knaben Wunderhorn*, III, 229 ff.

6 Bernard of Clairvaux, quoted in Pfannmüller, *Jesus*, pp. 189 and 191.

7 Cf. bibliography.

Bibliography

Achim, Ludwig, and Brentano, Clemens. *Des Knaben Wunderhorn* (reprint of the Heidelberg edition of 1819). 3 vols. Meersburg, 1928.

Adler, H. G. *Die Juden in Deutschland Von der Aufklärung bis zum Nationalsozialismus.* 2nd edition, Munich, 1961.

Agobard von Lyon. *Monumenta Germaniae Historica: Epistolae Karolingi Aevi*, III, 1899. Also, in Migne. *Patrologia Latina*, Vol. 54.

Baron, S. W. *A Social and Religious History of the Jews.* 3 vols. New York, 1929.

Baumgardt, D. *Great Western Mystics: Their Lasting Significance.* New York, 1961.

Benz, E. *Die christliche Kabbala.* Zurich, 1968.

Bergner, H. *Handbuch der kirchlichen Kunstaltertümer in Deutschland.* Leipzig, 1905.

Berthold von Regensburg. *Deutsche Predigten.* Edited by O. H. Brandt. Jena, 1924.

Boinet, A. *La Cathédrale de Bourges.* Paris, 1952.

Brière, G., and Vitry, P. *L'Abbaye de Saint-Denis.* Paris, 1948.

Buber, Martin. *Drei Reden über das Judentum.* Frankfurt, 1911.

Bühler, J. *Bauern, Bürger und Hansa.* Leipzig, 1929.

———*Fürsten und Ritter.* Leipzig, 1928.

Bühler, J. *Die Germanen in der Völkerwanderung.* Leipzig, 1925.

———*Die Hohenstaufen.* Leipzig, 1925.

———*Die Sächsischen und Salischen Kaiser.* Leipzig, 1924.

Cabaniss, A. *Agobard of Lyon.* Syracuse, N. Y., 1953.

Cahier, C., and Martin, A. *Catalogue des Manuscrits Français de la Bibliothèque Nationale.* Paris, 1896.

———*Monographie de la Cathédrale de Bourges Première Partie: Vitraux peints de Saint Etienne de Bourges.* 2 vols. Paris, 1841–44.

Chambers, E. K. *The Mediaeval Stage.* 2 vols. 1903.

Coulton, G. G. *Mediaeval Panorama: The English Scene from Conquest to Reformation.* New York, 1938.

Creizenach, W. *Geschichte des neueren Dramas.* 3 vols. 2nd edition, Halle, 1911–23.

Crosby, Sumner M. *L'Abbaye Royale de Saint-Denis.* Paris, 1953.

Dante Alighieri. *Le Opere di Dante: Testo Critico.* Firenze, 1921.

Dehio, G. *Geschichte der Deutschen Kunst.* 6 vols. Berlin, 1919 ff.

———*Handbuch der deutschen Kunstdenkmäler.* 5 vols. 1905–12. (New edition by E. Gall after 1935.)

———*Das Straßburger Münster.* Munich, 1922.

Detzel, H. *Christliche Ikonographie.* 2 vols. Freiburg, 1894–96.

Dibelius, M. *Jesus.* Berlin, 1939.

Döllinger, I. von. Die Juden in Europa, 1881. Reprinted in *Deutsche Akademie-Reden.* Edition of Fritz Strich. Munich, 1924.

Eckhart, Meister. *Predigten und Schriften.* Edited by F. Heer. Frankfurt, 1956.

Froning, R. *Das Drama des Mittelalters* (in *Kürschners Deutsche Nationalliteratur*). 2 vols. 1891 ff.

Gebhardt. B. *Handbuch der deutschen Geschichte.* 2 vols. Stuttgart, 1954–56.

Goldschmidt, A. *Die deutsche Buchmalerei.* Munich, 1928.

———*Die Elfenbeinskulpturen aus der Zeit der Karolingischen und Sächsischen Kaiser.* 4 vols. 1914–26.

Golther, W. *Die deutsche Dichtung im Mittelalter.* Stuttgart, 1922.

Graetz, H. *Geschichte der Juden von den ältesten Zeiten bis auf die Gegenwart.* 1873 ff.

Gregorius von Tours. *Zehn Bücher fränkischer Geschichte.* Translated by Giesebrecht.

Gregorovius, F. Der Ghetto und die Juden in Rom, 1853. *Wanderjahre in Italien,* Vol. I. 1890.

Grodecki, L. *Vitraux des Églises de France.* 1947.

Guardini, R. *Verantwortung: Gedanken zur jüdischen Frage.* Munich, 1952.

Haecker, T. *Tag- und Nachtbücher*. 2nd edition, Munich, 1947.
Harnack, A. von. *Augustin: Maximen und Reflexionen* (selected and translated works of St. Augustine). Tübingen, 1922.
Herrad von Landsberg. *Hortus Deliciarum*. Edited by Straub-Keller. Strasburg, 1879–99.
Hrabanus Maurus. Quoted in *Monumenta Germaniae Historica: Epistolae*, Vol. 5. 1899.
Jantzen, H. *Deutsche Bildhauer des 13. Jahrhunderts*. Leipzig, 1925.
Katz, S. *The Jews in the Visigothic and Frankish Kingdoms of Spain and Gaul*. Publications of the Mediaeval Academy, No. 28.
Kaznelson, S. *Jüdisches Schicksal in deutschen Gedichten* (an anthology). Berlin, 1959.
Kisch, G. *The Jews in Mediaeval Germany: A Study of Their Legal and Social Status*. Chicago, Illinois, 1949.
Klausner, J. *Jesus von Nazareth. Seine Zeit, sein Leben und seine Lehre*. 2nd edition, Berlin, 1934.
Kraus, F. X. *Geschichte der christlichen Kunst*. 3 vols. Freiburg, 1896–1908.
Künstle, K. *Ikonographie der christlichen Kunst*. 2 vols. 1928.
Lanckoronska, M. *Matthäus Gotthart Neithart*. Darmstadt. 1963.
Langosch, K. *Geistliche Spiele*. Darmstadt, 1957.
————*Hymnen und Vagantenlieder*. Darmstadt, 1954.
Laurent, Grimouard de Saint. *Les ivoires prégothiques conservés en Belgique*. 1912.
Liebe, G. *Das Judentum in der deutschen Vergangenheit*. Leipzig, 1903.
Longhust, M. H., ed. *Catalogue of Carvings in Ivory*. 2 parts. Victoria and Albert Museum, South Kensington, 1927–29.
Ludus de Antichristo. Editions:
Barrow, S. F., and Hulme, W. H. "Antichrist and Adam." *Western Reserve University Bulletin*. Cleveland, Ohio, 1925.
Froning, R. *Das Drama des Mittelalters*. 1891.
Langosch, K. *Geistliche Spiele*. 1959.
Meyer, W. *Abhandlungen zur mittelalterlichen Rhythmik*, Vol. 1. 1905.
Migne. *Patrologia Latina*, Vol. 113. 1855.
Maillet, G. *Manuscrits à peintures du XIII*e *au XVI*e *siécle*. Paris, 1896.
Mâle, E. *L'art religieux du XIII*e *siécle en France*. 1902
Maurer, W. *Kirche und Synagoge*. Stuttgart, 1953.
Michaelis, W. "Zum Ludus de Antichristo." *Zeitschrift für deutsches Altertum*. 1913.

Migne, J. P. *Patrologia Latina.* 221 vols. 1844–55.

Modder, M. F. *The Jew in the Literature of England to the End of the 19th Century.* 1939.

Moehlman, C. H. *The Christian-Jewish Tragedy.* Rochester, N. Y.

Molsdorf, W. *Christliche Symbolik der mittelalterlichen Kunst.* Leipzig, 1926.

———*Führer durch den symbolischen und typologischen Bilderkreis der christlichen Kunst des Mittelalters.* Leipzig, 1920.

Mone, F. J. *Lateinische Hymnen des Mittelalters.* 3 vols. Freiburg, 1853–55.

———*Schauspiele des deutschen Mittelalters.* 2 vols. 1846 ff.

Müllenhoff-Scherer. *Denkmäler deutscher Poesie und Prosa aus dem 8.–12. Jahrhundert.* Edited by S. Steinmeyer. 2 vols. Berlin, 1892.

Nohl, J. *Der Schwarze Tod: Eine Chronik der Pest.* Potsdam, 1924.

Otte, D. H. *Handbuch der Kirchlichen Kunst–Archäologie des deutschen Mittelalters.* 2 vols. 1883–84.

Pelka, O. *Elfenbeine.* 2nd edition, Berlin, 1923.

Pfannmüller, G. *Jesus im Urteil der Jahrhunderte.* 2nd edition, Berlin, 1939.

Pflaum, H. *Der allegorische Streit zwischen Synagoge und Kirche in der europäischen Dichtung des Mittelalters.* Archivum Romanum, 1934.

Pinder, W., and Hege, W. *Der Bamberger Dom und seine Bildwerke.* 3rd edition, Berlin, 1936.

Reiners, H., and Ewald, W. *Kunstdenkmäler zwischen Maas und Mosel.* Munich, 1921.

Sauer, J. *Symbolik des Kirchengebäudes und seiner Ausstattung in der Auffassung des Mittelalters.* 1st edition, Freiburg, 1902 (2nd edition, 1924). The articles "Kirche–Symbolik und Kunst" and "Synagoge in der Ikonographie" appear in *Lexikon für Theologie und Kirche.* Edited by Buchberger. Vol. V. (2nd edition, 1933) and Vol. IX (2nd edition, 1937). Freiburg in the Breisgau.

Schmarsow, A. *Italienische Kunst im Zeitalter Dantes.* Augsburg, 1928.

Schmitt, O. *Gotische Skulpturen des Freiburger Münsters.* 2 vols. Frankfurt, 1926.

Schoeps, H. J. *Jüdisch-Christliches Religionsgespräch in neunzehn Jahrhunderten.* 2nd edition, Frankfurt on the Main, 1949.

———*Jüdische Geisteswelt: Zeugnisse aus zwei Jahrtausenden.* Darmstadt, 1953.

Sedlmayr, H. *Die Entstehung der Kathedrale.* Zurich, 1950.

Seiferth, W. "The Veil of Synagogue." *Horizons of a Philosopher: Essay in Honor of David Baumgardt*, pp. 378–90. Leiden, 1963.

———*Zur Kunstlehre Dantes: Archiv für Kulturgeschichte.* XVII, 194–225, and XVIII, 148–67. 1927–28.

Stadler, E. *Dichtungen.* Hamburg, 1954.

Steeger, T. *Leo des Grossen sämtliche Sermonen.* 2 vols. 1927.

Swarzenski, H. *Vorgotische Miniaturen.* 1931.

Vesper, W. *Der deutsche Psalter.* Ebenhausen, 1914.

Walther von der Vogelweide. Edited by Pfeiffer-Bartsch. Leipzig, 1911.

Weber, P. *Geistliches Schauspiel und kirchliche Kunst in ihrem Verhältnis, erläutert an einer Ikonographie der Kirche und Synagoge.* Stuttgart, 1894.

Werfel, Franz. *Between Heaven and Earth.* New York, 1944.

———*Paulus und die Juden.*

Westwood. *Descriptive Catalogue of the Fictile Ivories in South-Kensingston Museum.* n.d.

Wolfskehl, K., and Von der Leyen, F. *Älteste deutsche Dichtungen.* Leipzig, 1920.

Young, K. *The Drama of the Mediaeval Church.* 2 vols. Oxford, 1933.

———"Ordo Prophetarum." *Transactions of the Wisconsin Academy of Sciences, Arts and Letters*, XX, 1 ff. Madison, Wisconsin, 1921.

Zunz, L. *Die synagogale Poesie des Mittelalters.* 1855. (Later edition, Frankfurt, 1920.)

Index